Working Couples

*the text of this book is printed
on 100% recycled paper*

Working Couples

Edited by Rhona Rapoport and Robert N. Rapoport
with Janice M. Bumstead

HARPER COLOPHON BOOKS
Harper & Row, Publishers
New York, Hagerstown, San Francisco, London

A hardcover edition of this book is published by Routledge & Kegan Paul Ltd. It is here reprinted by arrangement.

First HARPER COLOPHON edition published 1978

ISBN: 0-06-090594-8

80 81 82 10 9 8 7 6 5 4 3 2

Contents

Acknowledgments

The spadework for bringing together people and ideas to form this book was accomplished in 1976 collaboratively with Joseph Pleck, whose initiative with many of the contributors was instrumental in their early involvement in the work.

The book as it now appears is an effort to bring together experienced workers in a new field. It is not comprehensive. It is certainly not, we hope, the last word.

Rhona Rapoport
Robert N. Rapoport
Janice M. Bumstead

Contributors

WILLIAM ARKIN received his PhD from Washington University in 1972. He is currently lecturing in Sociology at San José State University, California. His research interests are primarily in social control and social deviance, on which he is presently writing a book. His more recent interests in sex-roles, adult socialization, and job sharing are the result of continued research in social change and its relationship to social control.

LOTTE BAILYN received her PhD in Social Psychology from Harvard University in 1956. She is at present Associate Professor of Organizational Psychology and Management in the Sloan School of Management of the Massachusetts Institute of Technology. She has published numerous articles and monographs on the mass media, on education and on the relations between work and family life.

MICHAEL BERGER is Assistant Professor of Psychology and Assistant Director of the Family Studies Laboratory at Georgia State University, Atlanta, Georgia. A community/clinical psychologist and family therapist, his major interests include dual-worker families, families with handicapped children, and the study of social networks.

JANICE M. BUMSTEAD is the Director of Marie Stopes House in London, England's oldest birth control clinic and now an alternative health-care centre. Born in England, she attended a convent school and trained as a nurse. From 1969 to 1975 she lived in the USA and developed several health projects in the universities and poor areas of Boston. She also worked as a co-therapist and holds a Master's degree in Education from Harvard University. She is an active partner in a two-career family.

MARCELLINUS P. J. M. DIJKERS was born in the Netherlands, 1947. He has an MA degree in Sociology from the Catholic University of Nijmegen, the Netherlands. At the time of writing he was PhD candidate at Wayne State University, Detroit, and Research Assistant at the Family

Study Center at the same university. Areas of interest are family, stratification, language, social psychology and methods of social research.

LYNNE R. DOBROFSKY received her PhD from St. Louis University in 1972. She is currently Assistant Professor of Sociology at Mills College, California. Prior to her most recent interests in job sharing as one alternate work pattern for couples as well as non-couples, her research interests have been in the family, on women, and more recently on sex-roles and the military with a special focus on the military wife and feminism and on masculinity and military socialization. Additionally, she is presently involved in doing evaluative research on innovative mathematics and computer science programs for women in higher education.

ELIZABETH DOUVAN is a Professor of Psychology and Program Director in the Institute for Social Research at the University of Michigan. She is co-author of *The Adolescent Experience* and *Feminine Personality and Conflict*.

AGNES FARRIS has a BA from Smith College, Northampton, Massachusetts, received in 1972, and in 1974 received her MS in Management from the Sloan School of Management, MIT, on Commuting Couples. Her article is based on her Master's thesis.

MARTHA FOSTER is Co-ordinator of Infant-Preschool Services, North Metro Children's Center, Atlanta, Georgia. She is also Director of the Family and Infant Project, a program for handicapped children aged from one to three and their families. Her major interest is in the relationship of family structure and functioning to the development of child behaviour.

DAN GOWLER. After spending fourteen years in industry, Dan Gowler obtained a mature students' state scholarship to Queen's College, Cambridge, and read Economics and Social Anthropology. Following this he worked as a Research Fellow at the Centre for Business Research (Manchester Business School), being concerned with the theoretical and practical problems presented by the design and selection of wage-payment systems. After holding a Senior Lectureship in Occupational Behaviour in the Manchester Business School, he moved to the Medical Research Council, Social and Applied Psychology Unit, University of Sheffield, as a Professorial Fellow, directing a research project on the evaluation of programmes of planned organizational change. He was co-editor (with K. Legge) of *Managerial Stress* and co-author (with K. Legge) of the *Report of the Organization of Local Marriage Guidance Councils*.

ERIK GRONSETH is Associate Professor at the Institute of Sociology,

Oslo University, Fellow of the Oslo Institute of Social Research, and has been a Visiting Lecturer at Case Western Reserve University, in the USA. His research, yielding numerous publications in professional books and journals, has been on the political role of women, seamen's wives and their families, socialization, and on family policy. He is currently working on alternative patterns of the distribution of economic responsibilities for child care.

CHARLES HANDY is Warden of St George's House, Windsor Castle. After a career with Shell International and Charter Consolidated, he joined the new London Business School in 1967 to become Professor of Management Development. In the past ten years his teaching, research and consulting interests have been concerned with the Design of Organization, the Education of Managers and the lives, families and careers of executives. He has published many articles on these topics, and a textbook for managers, *Understanding Organizations*.

KAREN LEGGE, formerly Lecturer in Organizational Behaviour at Manchester Business School, University of Manchester, England, is now engaged in full-time research into the evaluation of planned organizational change at the Medical Research Council Social and Applied Psychology Unit, University of Sheffield. Her previous research interests have concerned the theory of reward systems and the operation of labour markets, with particular reference to the relationship between status, effort and reward. Apart from papers in academic and management journals, she was co-editor (with D. Gowler) of *Managerial Stress* and co-author (with D. Gowler) of the *Report of the Organization of Local Marriage Guidance Councils*. She is also joint editor of *Personnel Review* (with Enid Mumford) and of *Journal of Management Studies* (with A. G. Lockett).

JOSEPH H. PLECK was, at the time of writing, Assistant Research Scientist at the Institute for Social Research at the University of Michigan. He is now Associate Director, Center for the Family, University of Massachusetts. He co-edited *Men and Masculinity*, and has written and lectured widely on men's roles and male liberation.

RHONA RAPOPORT is a Sociologist and Psychoanalyst, and Co-Director of the Institute of Family and Environmental Research. With her Co-Director she is author of *Dual-Career Families, Dual-Career Families Re-Examined, Leisure and the Family Life Cycle* and *Fathers, Mothers and Others*.

ROBERT RAPOPORT is a Social Anthropologist, and is currently Co-Director of the Institute of Family and Environmental Research. With his Co-Director he is author of *Dual-Career Families, Dual-Career Families*

Re-Examined, Leisure and the Family Life Cycle and *Fathers, Mothers and Others*.

MARY POTTER ROWE is Special Assistant for Women and Work to the President and Chancellor of the Massachusetts Institute of Technology, and Institute Ombudsperson. An economist by training (PhD, Columbia, 1971) she has worked with a number of research, consultancy and action programs, mainly in the field of equal opportunity for women and minority groups. Author and co-author of several books, monographs and articles in the field of child care, she is a mother of three children and member of a working couple with her husband, psychologist Robert Fein.

CONSTANTINA SAFILIOS-ROTHSCHILD was born in Greece, where she received her education through university level in Athens. Her degree in sociology was at Ohio State. She is Professor of Sociology and Director of the Family Research Center at Wayne State University. In 1977–8 she is Professor of Sociology, University of California, Santa Barbara. Editor of several professional journals in the family field and author of numerous monographs and scientific articles in the field of the comparative study of the family, her recent books include *Women and Social Policy* and *Love, Sex and Sex Roles*.

BARBARA STRUDLER WALLSTON is Associate Professor and Chairperson of the Psychology Faculty at George Peabody College for Teachers, Nashville, Tennessee. A personality and social psychologist, her major interests include dual-worker families, professional role models, and health locus of control.

KATHY WEINGARTEN is a clinical psychologist currently practising in the Boston area. She teaches a course on the family at Wellesley College and is a Research Associate at the Wellesley Center for Research on Women in High Education and the Professions. She and Pamela Daniels have just completed a report on their study of family timing, entitled *Now or Later? The Timing of Parenthood in Adult Lives*.

THE WORKING FAMILY PROJECT is a team of anthropologists, psychologists and sociologists working at the Center for the Study of Public Policy, Harvard University for the past three years. The members are Laura Lein (Principal Investigator), Jan Lennon (Administrator) and Maureen Durham, Gail Howrigan, Laura Lein, Michael Pratt, Ronald Thomas, Heather Weiss (research collaborators). All of the staff members but one are students or recent graduates of advanced degree programs at Harvard University. Maureen Durham is on leave from the University of Chicago. The Working Family Project has recently published a pamphlet for the PTA called 'Work and the American Family' and has produced an interim report, 'Work and the Family'.

Introduction

Why a Book on Working Couples?

This is a book about married couples who both hold paid jobs. We call such families dual-worker families. The contributors have studied the experiences of dual-worker families and have considered some of the issues confronting them. They discuss how some of these issues have arisen and analyse how they are being dealt with in a number of contexts.

Working couples, in meeting the challenges they face, are subject to constraints of various kinds and there are many who reject the pattern on these grounds. But, there are others who find and create devices for making the pattern work. We are concerned with discovering and clarifying some of the generic issues confronted, and learning which resolutions have been found satisfactory.

Why do working couples present any special issues? In pre-industrial times both men and women generally worked for the family subsistence; and even today it is normal in some occupations and professions to find husbands and wives working in close partnership. The reason it is a new issue is that many families outside the range of 'special cases', such as the small family shop or restaurant, are now attempting to operate this pattern and in new ways. The wife is no longer necessarily her husband's help-meet, counter-clerk, receptionist, hostess or whatever. She may have an independent job or career, and her earnings may be not only independent of his, but larger and more reliable. Five per cent of wives in intact marriages at this point earn more than their husbands, and if one considers couples where earnings are at a par—say within a category one way or the other—the current estimate is 20 per cent of couples in the USA. Many of these couples are finding that the new patterns do not fit very well with the way they were socialised, or with the way our society is organised.

Our society has evolved, as a dominant lifestyle, a 'conventional pattern' of sex-roles and division of labour between home and work. This conventional pattern, developed with industrialisation, has been characterised by a specialised division of labour in which only men have been defined as 'working'. A woman's place has been seen as in the home, removed as far from the workplace as the logistics of housing and transport allowed.

The male has been seen as the provider, the female as the one who cared for home and children. Initially this was seen as a privileged role, in which the wife was protected from a world in which women's participation was viewed as unsuitable and unnecessary.

In the last century and early part of this century, women's removal from the outside world of work and concentration in the home was seen as a reflection of what was 'right' and 'good'. It was seen as 'right' in terms of a presumed natural order of sexual division of labour; and 'good' in terms of the greater happiness and well-being for the family. Then, in the two World Wars women were brought into the labour force in unprecedented numbers, but, until the present decade, this remained defined as exceptional, and no fundamental restructuring of social roles and institutions occurred to give it continuity. It is only recently that there have been social and legal efforts to normalise the pattern. In so doing a number of problems are characteristically encountered.

One set of problems is in the minds and emotions of the individuals seeking to change their lifestyles. Reared with a conception of the 'normal' family pattern as one in which the male provider is 'head' of the household and the housewife is his helpmeet, it is difficult to think otherwise with any depth of conviction though the idea at a superficial level of equality for all is very modish.

Another set of problems relates to the social and cultural fabric of our society, which has been so structured that when any given couple departs from the conventional pattern they encounter resistances and strains of various kinds. These range from practical timetabling difficulties to difficulties associated with others' critical attitudes toward them in relation to deviating from expectations in specific situations.

For all these reasons the new pattern of working couples tends to be a stressful one, despite the fact that it has been to some extent legitimised and has recently achieved broader prevalence. In more and more households, including those with small children, both husbands and wives have paid jobs – over 40 per cent for recent USA figures and nearly as high in Britain. But though behavioural problems have changed, there are many lags in values and social institutions have not changed correspondingly. It is not national policy for women to work. In fact, strong *counter*-arguments based on selected data indicating potential damage to children and to marriages as a consequence of wives' working are widely heard. So, despite equal opportunity legislation, the occupational option is an easier one for males (where many social forces press for it) and more difficult for females (where many social forces militate against it). As a consequence many couples who both opt to work find it difficult. Some abandon the dual-work pattern; others sustain it but suffer a heavier emotional toll than is necessary; many couples are reluctant to try the pattern because of a distaste for possible criticism, a lack of social encouragement, and a fear of deleterious consequences in their personal lives.

We introduce here some specification of the issues which arise when couples decide to be 'working couples'. The contributors to the book provide a more detailed analysis of particular issues on the basis of their research.

A grasp of the general pattern of issues can be obtained by considering the framework in Figure 1.

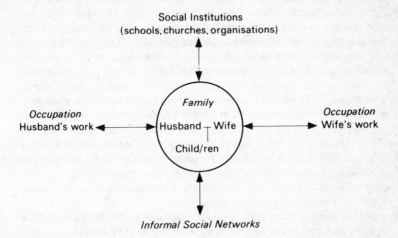

Informal Social Networks

The crucial structural difference between conventional families and dual-worker families is that in the latter both husband and wife sustain external links to occupations, whereas in the former it is only the husband. Considering the contributions in this framework, a clear picture of the place of each contribution emerges. We can also see the gaps as yet undealt with. We return to this in the final chapter.

Let us consider the issues in three groupings:

(a) Issues relating to linkages between family and occupations.
(b) Issues relating to relationships within the family.
(c) Issues relating to linkages between the family and non-occupational social institutions and networks.

Family and occupations

First, working couples are distinctive because both partners have linkages to the world of work, rather than only the husband. At work either or both may encounter hostility deriving from the impact of their dual-worker pattern on others. They may be felt to have an unfair economic or political advantage over other couples with a single earner. This may, for example, be particularly acutely felt by couples who choose to have children early in their marriage and are thereby put at a disadvantage in the mortgage market because their earnings cannot match comparably placed dual-worker couples.

The wife's boss may be sceptical about whether she can perform as well as a man, or whether she will stay on and be a reliable employee or drop out to have babies. Her colleagues may have low expectations of her participation at work, basing their attitude on the conventional viewpoint that it is impossible for women to combine the roles of parent and worker. Or, they may respond to her presence with stereotyped negative expectations, such as, she will introduce emotional difficulties to the work situation.

There are various responses to these negative encounters. Some women seek to prove themselves competent workers by not admitting when they are fatigued, or by overcompensating and becoming 'superworkers', allowing themselves less leeway than male colleagues – to prove that they can 'do it'. On the other hand, women may also derive satisfactions from their jobs comparable to those of men in the same sort of work. Increasingly, women have a work-role as part of their self-conception and, whatever part economic motives may play in taking and sustaining a job, women expect and find other satisfactions too.

Similar contrasts also hold, of course, for the men. Husbands in working couples may experience difficulties at work that might have been absent if their wives had been at home. If the husband in a working couple shares child-care responsibilities with his wife, he may, for example, pick up his child from some activity or take the child to the doctor. This means that family timetables intrude more into his work situation than they do for men whose wives attend to all of the family timetable co-ordination. If he is attending a meeting that goes on longer than expected, for example, he is faced with a dilemma. As a committed employee he has conventionally been expected not to be distracted by parenting obligations. If his workmates are not understanding, he may be teased, his 'manliness' impugned, and in extreme cases his job or career may suffer.

Relationships within the family

Typically, a working-couple family is involved in a pattern of activities which are different from those of the conventional family, and which create potentials for stress. The stresses may be resolved more or less satisfactorily. With the wife employed outside the home, the domestic tasks which are conventionally assumed to be accomplished by the housewife as unpaid, somewhat 'invisible' work, become problematic because in the time and with the energy she might have given to these tasks, she is at work in a paid occupation.

The conventional response to the new situation is to speak of the wife's 'two jobs'. One rarely hears, in this context, of the husband's 'two jobs' (unless he is 'moonlighting'). The implication is that if she wants to work, she should carry the overloads of work *plus* conventional domestic obligations. She works a 'double shift'.

Alternatively the husband may share the tasks conventionally defined as female; or the working couple may be assisted by a helper, who may be a grannie, a domestic helper, or any of a range of professional domestic-service workers. Many working couples use some combination of all of these.

But, while stresses and strains have received considerable attention, it should not be assumed that only trouble comes into the family as a consequence of this restructuring of occupational roles. The family that chooses the dual-working pattern, for whatever reason, is likely to derive additional rewards as well as incurring additional stresses. More money will usually be earned, though more services will usually have to be paid for. The wife may feel more fulfilled as a person, though this too is affected by the type of job she has and it is likely in any case to be tempered by the possibility that she may be more exhausted by the additional effort required.

One way that couples seek to minimise the strains on the intimate 'interior' of a family is to establish a new balance in their pattern of family and work commitments. If the husband does not recognise the importance of this but says, in effect, 'I want you to do whatever you want to do to be happy', adding explicitly or implicitly 'so long as it doesn't affect your attending to my needs', he is laying an emotional booby-trap for the relationship; particularly if his wife aims at a work commitment comparable to his.

The wife, too, may lay an emotional booby-trap in the couple relationship if she concentrates on attaining parity in work, hoping that the domestic parity will follow automatically.

On the other hand, there is no doubt that many of those who *over*-emphasise the difficulty of this pattern and reject it for that reason lose life opportunities for potential self-realisation which they, too, may regret in the future.

Perhaps more in the consciousness of young couples, particularly at the point of the arrival of the first child, is the issue of the possible harmful effects on the child of mother's work. Research on maternal deprivation conducted on institutionalised wartime babies separated from their mothers lent credence to the view that separation is a very real hazard. There is also no doubt that when children are neglected and when the pattern is associated with marital conflict, the growing child does not have an optimal environment for growth.

More recent research has indicated, however, that a much more differentiated view is required. It is now recognised that it is a fallacy to 'blame' such difficulties as abnormalities in child development and in social adjustment of adolescents on working mothers. Some babies are damaged by maternal separation, others are damaged by maternal over-involvement and from a learned incapacity to confront and deal with separations, which after all punctuate the life-cycle. Some ways of handling separations are beneficial, others harmful. When mothers work, child-parent contact may not, in fact, be eliminated or even reduced, only differently spaced and structured. The evidence available does not prove that mothers going out to work necessarily deprive their babies of needed emotional support. But we need much more knowledge and discussion on what conditions allow couples to work out a responsible and even beneficial pattern of parenting, so that separations and involvements can be structured so as to avoid the damaging situations.

The family and other social institutions

Many other social institutions, such as schools, are organised to complement the conventional family pattern. If a couple becomes a working couple issues continuously arise such as: Who will take the children to and from school? Who will wait for hours in the health centre during morning clinics, for the child's measles injection? How can the disapproval of the pattern expressed by teachers, doctors or social workers be dealt with? How can conventional-minded relatives and friends be dealt with? Rather than having them to turn to in distress, they are often experienced by dual-worker families as providing additional unwanted problems because they are critical figures against whom one must defend oneself. They may have a particularly powerful capacity to rouse feelings of guilt.

In a dual-worker family's relationships with other social institutions and with less formal social groups and networks the central dilemma seems to be how much energy to put into restructuring these relationships. They are needed as potential supports – and many of them; schools, hospitals and other service personnel are indispensable. In other instances – relatives, neighbours, friends – they represent valued human involvements. But, whether required for utilitarian purposes, or wanted for personal values, these relationships tend in the present state of affairs in our society to be generally unsupportive of the dual-worker family pattern – and therefore particular families who wish to operate the pattern run the risk of going one way or the other – toward total self-reliance (ultimately impossible), or toward total compliance with the conventional expectations of others (ultimately abandoning the pattern).

These then are a few of the problems which arise in the relationships of a working-couple family. In much of the earlier work in the field, the concentration was on the destructive potentials of this pattern. Fears were expressed that it would destroy the marriage, ruin the sex-life, emasculate the male and make the female 'hard' and aggressive. Fears were also expressed that it would damage the children.

Given the fact that there are proponents who emphasise the potential benefits of the pattern, and opponents who emphasise its potentially harmful consequences, it seems important at this point to review what can be learned from couples who have actually experienced the pattern.

The contributions of research

The papers presented in the chapters to follow are all based on research on working couples. Each contributes something to our understanding of a specific process important in establishing and operating the working-couple pattern.

We begin by examining a very concrete problem which couples must face as they seek to establish the pattern initially: finding two jobs. Michael Berger, Martha Foster and Barbara Wallston report on a study of American college graduates who seek to find jobs for both partners on leaving university. Professional and academic job markets are not usually set up for couples in which both partners wish to work. Such couples find little help from employers in exploring two job possibilities simultaneously. Jobs are offered to individuals, and if the partner is taken into account at all, the tendency is to assume that wives will adapt to their husbands taking the best possible job offered to him. Increasingly couples wish to arrange jobs which provide the best combination of opportunities for the couple. But when faced with time pressure and job scarcity, couples often feel pressured to make decisions which benefit one partner more than the other. One worker following the other is not usually preferred, but nevertheless it often occurs in forced choice situations. Couples vary in their capacity to deal comfortably with the interpersonal consequences of such asymmetries, but for people disposed to adopt this pattern, the existence of this kind of emotional backwash is a virtual certainty and needs to be confronted rather than denied.

Charles Handy, in a study of British middle managers and their wives, examines the specially *difficult situation confronting executives' families*, particularly when the executives are on their way up the organisation. The combination of 'greedy' organisational demands, and the conventional-mindedness of the sub-section of the population made up of men entering management, makes the working-couple option an infrequent one in this group. Where it is attempted, it tends to be a stressful one as it goes 'against the grain' of society, however much it may represent a modern idea.

Dan Gowler and Karen Legge have studied British managers' families in relation to occupational organisations, but in a different, more change-oriented perspective. In their paper on *hidden and open contracts* they specifically examine the implicit understanding among managers that a wife will act in support of the furtherance of her husband's career by not having one of her own. This assumption, which they call the 'hidden contract', has not usually had to be made explicit between the couple or the husband's employer, because it was usually accepted uncritically. As couples evolve more egalitarian conceptions of husbands' and wives' roles, the contracts are being made more open in the interests of dealing constructively with potential conflicts.

Constantina Safilios-Rothschild and Marcellinus Dijkers have studied a series of Greek couples in Athens in order to examine the whole question of how couples *handle unconventional asymmetries* which may arise in the lives of working couples. As Greeks are less totally oriented to earnings level as an index of personal worth than Americans, they thought it useful to compare the issues arising in Greek couples of different earnings levels, social class, and educational level with those known to exist in America. They found that in Greece, as in America, the lower-status couples are threatened by a wife's independence, and especially if there is any hint of the wife's superiority. A similar situation does not create as much tension in middle- or upper-class couples where the husbands apparently do not equate the higher status of their wives with a loss of masculinity. So, economic factors are important in both cultures, but they are important differently in that they combine with other factors to form specific situations in each society.

The Harvard Working Families Project team have examined the issues raised for the *division of labour between parents in dual-worker families with children.* Their study contained more blue-collar workers than some of the other studies. Families of this kind have been found to have particularly conventional sex-role models. In early phases of the trend toward increased prevalence of two-worker families it was widely assumed, particularly among blue-collar families, that the wife, if she wished to work, would do so primarily to earn extra money for herself – not as part of the basic economic provision structure of the family. Therefore, it was expected that she would simply add this to her conventional duties, continuing to carry the domestic and child-care responsibilities, perhaps with a little help from her husband. The Harvard team describe attempts of modern couples to alter this toward a more equal sharing of parenting.

Part of any restructuring of parental roles involves child care. Mary Rowe examines the issues involved in *choosing child care* in the modern American context, and describes some of the options now available and trends under way. Her analysis of social trends suggests the need for a more differentiated and flexible view of constructive approaches to sharing child rearing.

Sometimes, operating the working-couple pattern involves a still more radical adaptation. If a couple is determined to pursue both careers even if it means maintaining separate residences, they become what Agnes Farris calls a *commuting couple*. She studied a number of such couples in the USA, examining how couples make this decision, and the myths and realities of their experience with it.

Another structural option is examined by Erik Gronseth, who studied a series of Norwegian couples' experiments with *work sharing*. The couple together engage in a pattern whereby each shares a job outside the home (with the spouse or someone else) and also shares the work at home. Gronseth and his colleagues are convinced that this pattern, which is effectively a part-time occupational pattern, is the only way that working couples can manage without a level of stress which erodes the gains from being a working couple.

William Arkin and Lynne R. Dobrofsky look at a specific form of job sharing in a series of American west-coast couples who actually *share a single job*. This option is increasingly found in academic life, and may have a wider relevance once its problems and advantages are better understood.

Elizabeth Douvan and Joseph Pleck take up the problem of *separations* which often occur when couples pursue two work-careers. They see separation as a phenomenon which, though often stressful, may under some circumstances provide structural supports for the development of one or both partners. They provide illustrations of some of the circumstances under which such structured apartness provides an opportunity for growth and individuation while still remaining compatible with needs for intimacy and sharing.

Several of the essays highlight important aspects of relationship processes in working-couple families which are often overlooked. In her essay on *interdependence*, Kathy Weingarten examines the many different levels at which husbands and wives in working couples can mutually support each other and how this mutuality of support may be enhanced rather than undermined by the couple's equal standing in the world of work. Contrary to those who fear that the independence of working wives will automatically threaten the marital relationship, Weingarten shows that this depends on the couple's recognition of their interdependence and taking appropriate steps to make the concept of interdependence operate.

Lotte Bailyn considers some of the problems of *accommodation* that must occur in the relation between occupational and home life if the interdependence is to be possible for working couples. Occupational circumstances impose a variety of constraints. Bailyn analyses the force and implications of some of these, particularly as they are experienced by the

American managers and technologists she studied, and notes how a long-term time perspective is important as not only do situations change, but couples and their needs change through the life-cycle. It is therefore not appropriate to suggest mechanistic rules for accommodation.

In the final chapter, we review the picture derived from the contributions, note gaps, suggest the line of approach toward improving our understanding of the working couples' predicament, and suggest possible futures.

Key Processes

1

Finding Two Jobs[1]

Michael Berger, Martha Foster and
Barbara Strudler Wallston

Job-seeking is difficult for anyone who takes his or her work seriously. In addition to worrying about getting a job to meet one's financial obligations, applicants often have to offer themselves to potential employers again and again, to be evaluated, and to risk being rejected. And in this context, rejection often leads to feelings of worthlessness and depression – the individual's worth very often being measured by others and by herself/himself in terms of his/her marketability (Sennett and Cobb, 1972).

People take their work seriously for different reasons, and job-seeking means different things to people with different orientations toward their work. For some people, work is primarily a means of meeting financial obligations. For these people, the money is important and the work itself something which doesn't especially matter – 'it's just a job.' For other individuals, both financial payoff and the sense that one is good at one's work matters. For still others, work is a central concern of their lives, something they *must* do. For these people, work is a calling; in important ways, such individuals define themselves by their work.

While job-seeking is difficult for the individual applicant, it is an even more complicated process for the dual-worker couple. Such couples face the task of obtaining two positions that will (ideally) permit them to: (1) live in the same geographical area; (2) co-ordinate their schedules so that necessary household maintenance and child-care tasks can be carried out; (3) co-ordinate schedules so that they have free time to spend with each other, and time in which each spouse is free to do the things he or she likes to do individually; (4) get what they want from the particular job; and (5) satisfy their longer range career goals. Obviously, this isn't easy to do; the demands of work and family often conflict even in standard conventional situations, and for working couples the potential conflicts are multiplied. In the western world, dual-worker couples try to manage these conflicts within the context of a societal expectation that the careers of men are more important than the careers of women. Traditionally, men but not women are expected to be devoted to work. A man's status is primarily defined by his occupation, a woman's is not.

Traditionally, these conflicts were settled or diminished by a gender-based division of labor and responsibility within the household: husbands devoted themselves to their work and wives to the house and the children. This is probably still the solution most frequently found in our culture even where both parties have careers (Poloma and Garland, 1971; Oakley, 1974; Rapoport and Rapoport, 1971). But it is not a solution which meets the needs of all couples, and alternate solutions are being devised and explored.

There is need for such alternatives, since couples whose needs are not met by the traditional division of labor vary widely among themselves. Much of this chapter will be devoted to an exploration of how the experience of dual-worker couples in the job-seeking process is affected by the various factors which differentiate between such couples. We shall list and briefly discuss these factors:

1. All dual-worker couples do not share the same orientation toward work. In addition, within some dual-worker dyads, spouses share a similar orientation toward work; in others, they do not. A dual-worker couple may be composed of a spouse who views his/her work as a profession and a spouse who views his/her work as just a job. Or, both spouses may view their work as professional, in which case we call the couple a 'dual-career' couple.

2. The comparative status of the spouses within the marriage differs across dual-worker couples. In some couples, spouses hold equal-status position; in others, they do not.

3. Couples differ in whether, at any particular point in time, they regard the careers of both spouses as being of equal or of differing importance. For example, one couple may believe that both careers are equally important and therefore attempt to maximize the career development of both spouses. By contrast, another couple may see the husband's career as more important and will try to further his career first.

4. Dual-worker couples vary in terms of whether both spouses enter the job market at the same or at different times, and in terms of whether spouses are at similar or different career stages. Characteristically, men enter the labor market seeking full-time continuous employment at about the same point in their lives – after the completion of schooling or other training. Among working married women, there is much greater variation both as to when they enter the labor force and as to whether they work continuously. For example, it is quite common for married women to complete professional training and then to absent themselves from the labor force for years in order to bear and raise children, returning only after the children are in school. Such a pattern is almost unheard of among men. Behind this

difference in career patterns lie two widely held societal expectations: that all (or nearly all) men should work continuously and at
full-time employment, while women are not expected to do so; and
that child care should be carried out at home by the child's mother
(Bernard, 1971).

5. Working couples with children face more complex considerations in
job-seeking than do childless working couples.

The remainder of this chapter will examine the joint job-seeking process
in greater detail, paying particular attention to the ways in which the
factors we have just discussed affect the job-seeking process. We shall
begin by describing our own research. While it has been limited to studies
of job-seeking among dual-career couples, our discussion will focus upon
issues relevant to all dual-worker couples.

Two separate research studies exploring the job-seeking process in dual-
career couples were conducted in 1974-5. One study was a questionnaire
survey of 160 couples in which one spouse had recently obtained a doctor-
ate in either psychology or biological science and in which the other spouse
also held the terminal (highest) degree in his or her own field. The second
study involved interviewing 15 dual-career couples.[2] We required that
participants in both studies had jointly looked for jobs in the three years
prior to the study.

There were few prior data available to help us conceptualize the job-
seeking process. We began by looking at job-seeking as a process in which
couples first developed a set of guidelines as to how they would look for
jobs. For example: Would they apply all over the country or only in
certain geographic areas? Would they apply simultaneously or wait until
the other had obtained a job? How would they choose among the positions
which were finally offered?

For some couples, their initial strategies worked. For others, however,
their initial set of guidelines failed to work; they either were unable to
obtain acceptable positions or they had second thoughts about initial
agreements. For example, a husband who had agreed to let his wife decide
where they would move found that he was, in fact, unwilling to follow her
when the situation demanded it. In such cases, couples were likely to have
to develop new strategies. Given this conceptualization of the job-seeking
process, we were interested in the factors couples took into account as
they developed their job-seeking strategies, in the actual strategies which
couples employed, in the circumstances which caused couples to change
their strategies, and in the final job-seeking strategies adopted by couples
who did change their guidelines.

One important factor which greatly complicated the job-seeking process
was the timing of the final decision. In our thinking about the job-seeking
process we had assumed that at the point where the couple made a final

decision, all interesting jobs that had been available to them would still be available and the task would simply involve the choice among them. However, the job market, particularly when there are few jobs and many applicants, does not work that way. Rather, decisions about whether to accept or reject a particular job often have to be made before the relevant information about other potential opportunities is available. While the timing of job offers may well be a problem for individual applicants, it is more likely to cause difficulties for dual-worker couples who must co-ordinate their decisions. Indeed, over half the couples we studied indicated that this had been a problem for them.

In addition to the issues just raised, our personal experiences as members of dual-career couples seeking jobs led us to examine several other questions that we felt to be relevant. One of these was the issue of the amount and kinds of support available to dual-career couples during the job-seeking process. We were struck, during our own job-seeking experiences, by the fact that there seemed to be no norms for handling the job-seeking process as a couple. This was upsetting and stressful to us, but when we turned to colleagues for support and guidance they seemed confused about how to respond. We had all learned during professional training that each individual should seek the best possible position. No one, however, seemed to know how a professional spouse fit into the picture. In particular, how were we to deal with conflict that arose when the choice of the best position of one spouse would preclude the other spouse's choosing his/her best position? Additionally, we found that although the uncertainties of seeking employment created stresses and tensions that usually would be shared with one's spouse, the experiences we were having while job-seeking made it difficult for us to seek support from each other. When both spouses are feeling stressed and a major source of the stress is the legitimate needs of the other person, that person isn't likely to be an available source of comfort. It is hard to side with your spouse against yourself. It is also difficult to feel good about standing in your spouse's way. So we were very concerned about the support which couples sought out and received while job-seeking, and in the effects of the job-seeking process on other aspects of the marriage.

In our research, the various initial job-seeking decision rules which couples used were classified by the researchers into three categories: (1) traditional; (2) non-traditional; and (3) egalitarian. Strategies in which the wife followed the husband, that is, in which husbands first located a position and then wives looked in the same area, we classified as traditional. Strategies in which husbands followed wives we considered non-traditional. Several different strategies were considered to be egalitarian. For example, in some marriages each spouse independently looked for jobs and then the couple accepted the best joint option. In others, the spouses applied as a unit to the same employers or in the same geographic area.

And still other couples alternated as to whose career would take precedence, following a strategy of 'this time, we will go where you want to go and next time we'll go where I want.'

Slightly over half the *initial* decision rules were classified as egalitarian. Among those couples who did not adopt egalitarian strategies, women were much more likely to follow men than the reverse. However, only a quarter of the final decision rules were egalitarian. For their final decision, most of the couples chose the traditional strategy. What had happened during the job-seeking process to cause this change?

The major cause of this change seemed to be the character of the job market. Many of the couples who ultimately chose a traditional decision said that they had done so because only the male had been offered a job at the time they had to make a decision. These couples attributed their decision not to their own desires but to situational factors. Had the job market permitted it, they would have maintained their egalitarian strategy. Other data support the validity of this interpretation of their behavior. As part of the questionnaire, we included several simulated job-seeking incidents which required the spouses to choose among several possible decisions. In response to the simulated incidents, a high proportion (three-quarters) of the subjects chose egalitarian strategies. When they changed to non-egalitarian strategies, they did so in response to the situational pressures of time and the nature of the job market.

Couple responses to the simulated incidents seem consistent with their actual job-seeking behavior. Couples might want to follow an egalitarian strategy but found themselves with only one job offer, usually for the male. Thus, they were forced to choose between adopting a traditional strategy or facing the possibility that neither spouse would find a job. However, to outsiders who would be aware only of the choice made and not of the process by which the choice was made, it might look as if the couple had preferred the traditional decision. The issue of how the decision looks to others is important beyond the relevance to the couples themselves. Employers, observing such behavior, have often justified the non-employment or under-employment of married women on the grounds that these women are not as devoted to their own careers as men and will sacrifice them to follow their husbands. Our data suggest that, in part, it is the nature of the job market which gives credence to this employer belief: given a tight job market in which men are more likely to get jobs, married women who strongly value their own careers may nevertheless end up following their husbands, despite the fact that they *are* as committed to their careers as their husbands are, and that they do not make the sacrifice so readily, but only under duress.

Let us examine the stresses involved in this joint job-seeking process for dual-worker couples. One such stress is the likelihood that couples may need to deal with issues of competition and power within the marriage.

The very need to work out a job-seeking strategy, to decide how the differing demands of the two work-careers are to be reconciled, is likely to make the issue of power within the marriage salient. Power conflicts are especially salient for couples in which both careers are seen as being of equal importance and in which both spouses are devoted to their work. For these couples, unless it is possible to obtain positions which advance the careers of both spouses, the success (career advancement) of one spouse is likely to be at the expense of the other. Both our studies and previous studies of dual-career couples (Holmstrom, 1972) have found this to be a common predicament.

Moreover, since both spouses are heavily invested in their careers, giving in to one's spouse and giving up on one's own career advancement is likely to be viewed as a loss of professional status. People seem to assume that if one is a *real* professional, one will *not* give up on one's career advancement. Individuals in dual-career marriages have commented that deciding to limit their own career advancement by following their spouse has meant that their colleagues take them and their work less seriously. And for individuals who define themselves through their work, the loss of work-related status is a serious matter. The difficulties of this situation were well put by one woman in our study: 'I question the viability of (traditional) marriages when two individuals have a strong career commitment. In our case we decided not to live apart since how can a relationship be maintained with one member 3,000 miles from the other? So, I went with my husband. Yet, I felt a high degree of resentment and hostility having to "give up everything" and seek a job elsewhere.'

This situation is even further complicated for couples in which the wife's career is given precedence. It is rare for this to happen, and even rarer for the couple to acknowledge that they have chosen to do this (Poloma and Garland, 1971). Indeed, several women in the questionnaire study noted that one satisfying aspect of the job-seeking process for them was in discovering that their husband 'really was egalitarian.' No man in our study made a similar comment about his wife.

It is rare for couples to acknowledge that they have chosen to give the wife's career precedence because deferring to one's wife's career conflicts with traditional views of acceptable masculine behavior (Rosen, Jerdee and Prestwich, 1975). In our interview study, one of the subjects was a man who had resigned his position to follow his wife and who had not obtained a job in the subsequent year and a half. Personally, both he and his wife were content with the decision that he follow her. However, because of the stigma attached to his being unemployed and a house-husband, both he and his wife maintained the fiction, with their families of origin, that he was employed. When their families visited, he would take them to her office telling them it was his. The stigma attached to his condition was made clear in the remark of a colleague who knew the couple: 'Of course, any man who would choose not to work can't be worth much sexually.' And dual-worker couples, themselves, are not immune to these societal judgments. As one woman wrote: 'We considered that I would apply for jobs and my husband would accompany me, but in the end I rejected this due to the personality and ambition of my husband whom I knew could never be happy in a temporary position or not having a job.'

Another set of stressful issues related to joint job-seeking is the negotiation of satisfactory divisions of labor with regard to household tasks and child rearing. Given societal attitudes concerning the relative importance of work for men and women, it is not surprising that the common pattern is for the wife to co-ordinate her schedule and career around her husband's work schedule and career.

This pattern is particularly prevalent when children are present in the family. As we noted earlier, mothers are expected to stay home and care for their children. Women who conform to this expectation remove themselves from the labor market for several years. Absence from the labor market increases the likelihood that when the woman returns to work she will return to lower paid and lower status employment than her husband. While she has been home caring for the children, he has (ideally) been advancing his career. Thus, many women with children, even though they value their work highly, come under new pressure to follow their husbands in the job-seeking process because their husband's earnings are now so much greater than their own. To put the wife's career first in such instances would mean that the family would have to lower its standard of living. Furthermore, if, as occurs commonly, the wife requires training before she can return to work, this means that the family must incur the additional expense of paying for her training while she is not earning anything. As one woman in this circumstance put it: 'My husband thinks it is fine for me to have a career – so long as it doesn't cost him anything.' In addition to the increased financial burden, the husband may anticipate a loss in her services and attentions as a consequence of his wife's divided allegiance between family and career. And, to complicate the situation even further, in a society in which the status of men is primarily defined by their success as providers, a woman's desire to return to work may be interpreted by her husband as an indication that he has failed in his major family role, especially if he is frustrated or stifled in his own job. Men with such feelings are unlikely to be supportive of their wives' returning to work. In addition, for some women, children's resistance to their going out to work dampens their enthusiasm for job-seeking. Children who have been accustomed to a full-time 'homemaker-mother' often resent their mother's 'abandoning the hearth,' although this may depend on the age of the children. There are likely to be many women who wanted to return to work earlier than they actually did, but did not because of the opposition of their husbands or children.

A further consequence of the expectation that mothers will assume primary responsibility for child care is that wives are generally expected to arrange their work schedules around the needs of their children. Even mothers who work outside the home characteristically devote large amounts of time to child care, arranging for sitters or day-care placement, taking children places, responding to illnesses or emergencies involving the children, etc. This child-care responsibility greatly limits the ability of these women to commit themselves to a full-time work schedule, particularly a schedule that might prove unpredictable or require long stretches of work at a time. Two women in our study sum up these difficulties:

> My husband received his Ph.D. in the Fall of 1973. Our first child was born one month before he finished. We moved to . . . that Fall where my husband accepted a post-doc. I was unemployed at the time, but planning to find a part-time teaching position. I would have liked a full-time faculty appointment, but felt *guilty* about leaving the baby full-time. Under the circumstances, I found a most satisfactory pattern – a half-time assistant professorship at . . . college.

> Most of our present and past job-seeking problems stem from the presence of the child rather than the willingness on the part of one of us to accommodate to the other's professional wishes. *However*, there is the underlying problem – brainwashed into both of us that 'woman's place is tending baby, and man's making the money' – therefore, I am the one who arranges my professional employment around the baby care.

One alternate pattern in this regard is interesting. In a recent study of dual-worker couples, Laura Lein and her colleagues (Lein *et al.*, 1974) found that many couples, in order both to divide child-care tasks more fairly and to ensure that both parents would have time to spend with the children, had arranged to work on different time-shifts so that one spouse would be home at any given time. This kind of egalitarian arrangement is related to how spouses view the relative importance of work and family. For spouses who view work as a financial necessity rather than personal commitment it is relatively easy to be purely supportive of each other's job-seeking endeavors. Under such circumstances, the wife's work will be seen as a way of expressing interest in the family rather than as a source of actual or potential competition to the husband's work. Among dual-career couples, the wife's work is more likely to be thought of as competing with the husband's work and spouses are therefore likely to have ambivalent feelings about each other's career endeavors. This does not rule out for dual-career families the kind of arrangement described by Lein and her colleagues but it makes it less likely.

A related factor which increases the likelihood that women in dual-worker couples will subordinate their careers to those of their husbands is the different importance placed upon family matters in the socialization of men and women. It has been widely noted that only women are expected to integrate their work and family lives. Men are permitted to specialize, to invest solely in work-roles (Bernard, 1974; Coser and Rokoff, 1971; Pleck, 1975). The fact that working women are more likely to assume primary child-care responsibility is one consequence of this difference in socialization. Another consequence of this difference in socialization is the greater amount of time spent by women in household maintenance tasks (Berger, Foster and Wallston, 1975; Bryson, Bryson, Licht and Licht, 1976; Oakley, 1974). In a recent study of professional couples in psychology, Bryson and her colleagues (1976) noted that while husbands married to working wives assume no greater amount of household responsibilities than do husbands married to non-working wives, working wives do assume less responsibility for household tasks than non-working wives; this is because they hire other people to do the household chores.

To summarize our discussion of the decision made during the job-seeking process, we note that most couples initially chose either egalitarian or traditional strategies. However, in response to a job market which often did not permit couples to obtain two acceptable positions, and in response to the need to make a decision at a specific time, many couples had to decide which career was to be given precedence. Generally, this decision was a traditional one, in favor of the husband's career, partly because husbands were more likely to be offered jobs, partly because husbands were likely to hold higher-paying positions, partly because wives were more likely to feel and be responsible for child care, and partly because couples found it hard to act against the societal expectation that the careers of men are more important than the careers of women. Despite these factors, one quarter of the couples made egalitarian final decisions. Many others indicated that if the job market had been less tight, they, too, would have chosen strategies that advanced both careers.

It is important to remember that most of the couples we studied were young, and married for the first time. Our findings might have been different had we studied a larger number of older couples, for the life-cycle tasks facing younger and older couples and their history and socialization are different. Younger couples, especially those entering the labor market at the same time, are establishing a lifestyle. Older couples who are jointly job-seeking frequently must relinquish prior assumptions about roles and must alter an already established lifestyle.

We need also to remember that the job-seeking decision discussed earlier is based upon two prior decisions, namely, that the couple will remain married and will live together. A small number of couples in our sample chose to abandon these assumptions. Some accepted positions requiring that they live apart from their spouse; others divorced. We have little information about couples who choose these alternatives. However, we think it requires extraordinary work commitment to choose to live separately from one's spouse in order to hold a job one likes, and that it is easier for couples without children than it is for couples with children (but see chapter 7).

We need now to briefly consider the issue of emotional support during the job-seeking process. Dual-worker couples need support because they have a lifestyle which departs from societal expectations about the 'proper' roles for married men and women (Rapoport and Rapoport, 1971). For reasons we have mentioned earlier, it is often difficult for members of dual-worker couples to obtain support from their spouses while job-seeking. Nevertheless, in our studies we found that most couples reported that the only person from whom they sought support was their spouse. The great majority of the dual-career couples in our study knew no other dual-career couples, couples who would be most likely to understand and sympathize with their predicament.

The job-seeking process is different and more difficult for dual-worker couples than for couples in which only one spouse works. Dual-worker couples must co-ordinate their job-seeking efforts and must search for positions which will allow them to manage the family tasks that are usually taken care of by the 'wife,' a person whose primary if not exclusive interest is the home and family (Oakley, 1974). Dual-career couples must deal with the competition and hurt feelings that are likely to arise when the career of one spouse is limited by the career of the other. At workshops we have conducted for dual-career couples, we found that issues around support are important to many couples.

At the same time there *are* satisfactions for dual-worker couples in the job-seeking process. Many couples in our study reported feeling good about locating two acceptable positions. Further, a number of individuals said that they were proud of the way in which they and their spouse had sought positions; they were proud that they were able to take both their career interests and the career interests of their spouse seriously. Lastly, dual-worker couples often comment that they are more interesting and easier to live with when they have jobs which they like.

How can the job-seeking process be eased for dual-worker couples? Our suggestions, based on the research we have reported, fall into three broad categories: (1) changes in institutional procedures; (2) provisions of more support for dual-worker couples; and (3) changes in socialization.

An increase in the number of jobs available would obviously be helpful to dual-worker couples. Needed also is much greater flexibility in the types of employment which are available and which are rewarded. For example, an increase in the number of part-time jobs and in the benefits paid to part-time employees would be beneficial to individuals who wish both to work and to be at home a substantial amount of the time. Similarly, increased acceptance of the practice of a couple sharing a job, that is, each spouse working half-time at it, would aid those couples who wished to combine work and family in this manner. Obviously, for this to happen, the usefulness of anti-nepotism rules (rules restricting the employment of members of the same family in the same institution) would have to be reconsidered. This is beginning to occur. Greater willingness to accept the fact that there is no 'right' age at which to enter training or at which to begin full-time employment would help women who wished to bear and raise children before working full-time and would be useful also to men and women who did not or could not definitively choose a career in their late teens or early twenties. Also helpful to these individuals would be some sort of economic subsidy for persons who require training relatively late in life so that the cost of such training would not be burdensome to their families.

Other institutional changes that would be helpful would be for government or industry to provide more child-care and home maintenance services; it is clear that the necessity of juggling such tasks with career demands is often difficult for dual-worker couples. Suggestions in this regard are found in the work of Rapoport and Rapoport (1971) and Oakley (1974).

We also need ways to reduce the loneliness and the sense of not being understood experienced by many dual-worker couples. So long as one spouse's career is likely to be constrained by the career of the other, sources of support available to both spouses *outside* the marriage are necessary. Increased awareness on the part of the public of the prevalence of dual-worker families and of the difficulties they encounter should be helpful in this regard. It should increase the likelihood that dual-worker couples will feel less deviant and less alone. Greater knowledge about dual-worker couples should intensify the demand for changes in institutional practices that would help these couples. Further, increased knowledge about dual-worker issues should help dual-worker couples correctly identify the sources of their strain, should help them stop blaming themselves or each other for problems caused by institutional constraints or biased socialization patterns. Increased knowledge should also help dual-worker couples deal more explicitly and more planfully with the issues that either are or will be facing them. Finally, by making the dual-worker lifestyle more of a public matter, increased knowledge about dual-worker issues should make it easier for dual-worker couples to seek out other dual-worker couples for advice and support.

Clearly, we think that many of the problems encountered by dual-worker couples in the job-seeking process are a function of the way in which men and women are socialized to think about work and family. Men, to be specific, are socialized *not* to think much about work and family, but to define themselves by their work. Indeed, work is the means by which they fulfill their family obligations of being a 'good provider'

(Mortimer, Hall and Hill, 1976; Pleck, 1975). Women, in contrast, are brought up to orient toward their family and, if they work at all, to subordinate their work interests to the interests of the family.

Essentially, then, connecting up one's career, one's marriage, and one's family involves a series of trade-off's, decisions and energies. It is the rare person who has the resources to care for each as much as he would like. Changes in the societal orientation toward work and career are required. One such change is simple: we need to stop telling women that they should not devote themselves to their work if they wish to, and we need to stop telling men that they must devote themselves exclusively to their work. Secondly, we need to make it more possible to connect the structures of the work world to the concerns of private (family) life. At present, it is hard to integrate these worlds. Professionals work 60–80 hour weeks carrying out the dictates of their professional training that work is paramount. Working-class men show their love for their wives and children by taking on extra jobs to earn more money to provide better for their families (Sennett and Cobb, 1972). The effects are similar: the men are rarely at home and are thus virtually inaccessible to their wives and children.

To put it mildly, the kinds of changes we are proposing are not simple. But they are possible, and they are necessary if dual-worker couples, who are increasing in number, are to have a better chance of utilizing their talents fully and of uniting their public and their private lives.

Notes

1 The assistance of Janet B. Franzoni, Sally F. Hughes and Larry Wright is acknowledged with gratitude. Thanks are also due to Michael O'Shea and Joyce Moore for their comments.
2 Fuller descriptions of these studies are available in the Wallston, Foster and Berger, and Berger, Foster and Wallston papers cited below. The former of these studies was supported in part by Biomedical Sciences Support Grant (FR-RR07087) from the General Research Support Branch, Division of Research Resources, Bureau of Health Professions, Education and Manpower Training, National Institutes of Health. The latter study was supported in part by funds from the Sponsored Research Office of Wichita State University, Wichita, Kansas.

Bibliography

Berger, M., Foster, M., and Wallston, B. (1975), 'Dual-career couples: Job-seeking strategies and family structure,' paper presented at the Annual Meeting of the American Psychological Association.
Bernard, J. (1971), *Women and the Public Interest*, Chicago: Aldine.

Bernard, J. (1974), *The Future of Motherhood*, Baltimore: Penguin.

Bryson, R., Bryson, J., Licht, M., and Licht, B. (1976), 'The professional pair: Husband and wife psychologists,' *American Psychologists*, 31 January.

Coser, R., and Rokoff, C. (1971), 'Women in the occupational world: Social disruption and conflict,' *Social Problems*, 18 April.

Holmstrom, L. (1972), *The Two-Career Family*, Cambridge, Mass.: Schenkman.

Lein, L., Durham, M., Pratt, M., Schudson, M., Thomas, R., and Weiss, H. (1974), 'Final Report: Work and family life,' National Institute of Education Project No. 3-3094, Cambridge, Mass.: Center for the Study of Public Policy.

Mortimer, J., Hall, R., and Hill, R. (1976), 'Husbands' occupational attitudes as constraints on wives' employment,' paper presented at the Annual Meeting of the American Sociological Association.

Oakley, A. (1974), *The Sociology of Housework*, New York: Random House.

Pleck, J. (1975), 'Work and family roles: From sex-patterned segregation to integration,' paper presented at the Annual Meeting of the American Sociological Association.

Poloma, M., and Garland, T. N. (1971), 'The myth of the egalitarian family: Familial roles and the professionally employed wife,' in A. Theodore (ed.) *The Professional Woman*, Cambridge, Mass.: Schenkman.

Rapoport, R., and Rapoport, R. N. (1971), *Dual-Career Families*, Baltimore: Penguin. Out of print. Second edition, *Dual-career Families Re-examined* (1976), London: Martin Robertson; New York: Harper & Row.

Rosen, B., Jerdee, T., and Prestwich, T. (1975), 'Dual-career marital adjustment: Potential effects of discriminatory managerial attitudes,' *Journal of Marriage and the Family*, 17 January.

Sennett, R., and Cobb, J. (1972), *The Hidden Injuries of Class*, New York: Random House.

Wallston, B., Foster, M., and Berger, M. (1975), 'I will follow him: Myth, reality, or forced choice?' paper presented at the Annual Meeting of the American Psychological Association.

2

Going Against the Grain: Working Couples and Greedy Occupations

Charles Handy

Our research with middle managers developing their careers toward senior management at the London Graduate School of Business Studies has suggested the need for a cautious approach to the advocacy of this pattern for all and sundry. For those working in what Coser has called 'greedy institutions', as do most managers in contemporary industrial society, the idea may not only be unattractive as a way of combining their occupational and familial lives, but it may embroil them and their wives in conflicts which they neither desire nor can easily avoid.

The research on which this paper is based differs from most of the others in this volume, in that it does not start with working couples or with a series of couples whose values and goals move them toward a search for ways of making the dual-worker family viable. On the contrary, it starts in a research project on managers and their families, a sub-group in our society which is amongst the most conventional-minded socially, and one in which any attempt to establish the working-couple pattern is clearly 'going against the grain' of the norms and expectations prevailing in the parts of society in which people of this kind live and work.

Because *even* managers live in a society in which there are powerful social trends in the direction of equal education, equal opportunity and egalitarian division of labour generally, it is to be expected (and we found) that *some* of the managers and their wives attempted to operate a working-couple structure despite the obstacles and constraints confronting them in their particular sub-sector of society. It is partly because their predicament is such a difficult one, and partly because they are still so numerous and important as members of our society, that the examination of our data from the point of view of the interest in working couples is felt to be more generally useful.

We studied 23 couples in which the husband was a manager. Of these, only four could be described as 'working couples'. All were career executives in large organizations or institutions.

When we combine the results of this research with the studies of the Pahls, Bailyn, Rapoports and others, a picture begins to emerge of the career requirements of middle and senior managers in our industrial corporations:

(a) Managers are expected to be highly committed to their jobs and to the organization, particularly if they want to advance.

(b) To survive in these competitive organizations can mean to strive to advance. It is not just a matter of personal preference – one may have to run just to stand still.

(c) Social norms, rightly or wrongly, still push the male into the main work-role, and the women into the back-up caring functions for husband and children.

(d) Couples who accept and conform to these norms and expectations go 'with the grain' of social forces in their occupational environment.

(e) Couples who go against the social grain in attempting to fashion full working lives for both partners when one is in a 'greedy occupation' have a different, probably greater set of strains and conflicts to deal with.

In the discussion that follows there is no attempt to prescribe one pattern of marriage rather than another. What seems right and proper for one couple will seem strange and stressful for another. But our data indicate that the working-couple option in marriages where the men are in mid-managerial career is a tough one, particularly if there are children. The wives in this study who sustain an occupation outside the home do so because it fulfils their needs as individuals. But the costs are evident, and the difficulties of doing so in a family where the husband is an ambitious manager make this sub-group a smaller one than amongst many other occupations.

The research in question[1] was exploratory, tentative and limited in its scope. We interviewed the couples, all with career executive husbands. But within this context, definable *marriage patterns* emerged.

The marriage patterns that we constructed were based on expressed attitudes or dispositions of the individuals involved. Each individual in the study was asked to complete the Edwards Personal Preference Schedule (EPPS). When decoded this standard attitude measurement device produces scores on fifteen attitude dimensions, the most useful of which were, for us, Achievement, Dominance, Affiliation and Nurturance.

We plotted these scores against the standard median scores of the EPPS, combining them to form four quadrants as shown in figure 2.

In other words, the individual who had combined scores on Achievement and Dominance which were higher than the standard median for the EPPS would be in the top half of the diagram. Higher than median scores on Affiliation and Nurturance combined would push him into the left-hand half. The individual with high scores on all four would, therefore, find him or herself in quadrant A. In this way we could plot every individual onto this matrix in a way which represented their expressed attitudes on the four selected dimensions. We then invented the titles for each quadrant.

Quadrant A we called Involved. These individuals had high needs to achieve and dominate, but also had high social needs. They wanted to belong to and be part of a group or strong relationship. The executives in this were often in staff roles or in the civil service.

Quadrant B we labelled Thrusting. This quadrant contained the most visibly successful of the males. They are high achievers with a need for dominance and low scores on Affiliation and Nurturance, implying that they are happy to act on their own, with less sensitivity to the group. This group contained the bulk of the executives in our sample.

Quadrant C contains the Existentialists – the loners. They have little desire to control others or to look after others. They are inner-directed, not particularly ambitious, but set their own standards for their lives.

Quadrant D are the Supportive Caring people who get their satisfactions from looking after others and belonging, rather than dominating. Many of the executive wives fell into this quadrant, only two of the men.

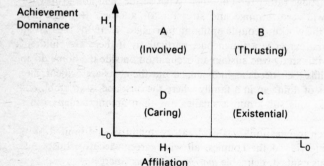

It should be emphasized that the patterns found reflect the occupational group (managers) and context (advanced management training programme). Had they been social workers, or librarians or any other group or counterpart the pattern might have been different.

To arrive at the *marriage patterns* we combined the husbands' orientations with the wives'. There are sixteen logical possible sets, but in fact only eight of the possible patterns were represented in our sample. B–D was the most common (a 'thrusting' man with a 'caring' wife). There were six of these. This is the stereotypical conventional pattern, and in this series none were 'working couples'. Working couples were, however, found in the next three patterns. In order of frequency in the sample these were:

B–B (two Thrusters)
A–D (Involved husband and Caring wife)
A–A (two Involved)

We would not of course wish to maintain that a whole relationship can be defined in terms of these few attitudes or dispositions. In fact, our study went on to investigate how each individual found, or did not find, an outlet for their most prominent characteristics. But we did find very distinct differences between the major marriage patterns pointed to by the scores on these four attitudes. The balance of 'Thrusting' or 'Caring' inclinations in each of us at any point in our lives has an effect on the way we manage the intimate relationship of marriage.

In the sample of managers and their wives that we studied, we found that the patterns differed:

in the way in which the relationship first started;
in the way roles were defined within the relationship;
in the priority given to the different activity areas of their lives;
in the ways relationships with others (children, friends, relations) were
    seen and handled;
in the way any problems or tensions were handled.

During the research we not only asked each couple to fill in questionnaire forms dealing with their own backgrounds, their current way of life and their perceptions of themselves as well as their general attitudes, but we also visited the family at home and observed how they lived.

Let us look at the principal marriage patterns in turn and explore their implications for working couples.

Pattern 1 B–D A thrusting husband and a caring wife

This pattern, the most frequent in our sample, is the conventional sex-role-stereotyped one. The husband works and the wife minds the home. She wants him and the children to be happy. His achievement and success, up to a point, are her goals as well. She concentrates her activities around the home, the husband/wife relationship, the family, and their social network. Role conceptions are clear and each partner knows what is expected. The husband is expected to help in the house and to take major policy decisions concerning it, but the wife is operationally in charge at home, just as he is in charge in the work arena. The problems they share are family problems: budgeting, children or mobility. She is unlikely to want to take a job herself unless there is a special need for money, e.g. for a family project of some kind. In such a case she tries to find work which pays as well as possible without being too demanding on time and energy. The husband tends to resent her working and discourages it. Since it is only done for money it must be seen as temporary or it would imply a failure on his part. The wife tends to be generally supportive of her husband in his work, although she does not show too much interest or involvement in its details. It is not a shared arena. One wife in the sample, a very supportive one, did not in fact know what her husband's job was, although she did know the name of his employers. She would have readily moved home if his work demanded it. The husband's need to dominate and achieve is no problem to the caring wife, particularly if he satisfies these needs in the work arena. The wife's task, as she sees it, is to absorb her own problems and those of managing the family, and not burden her husband. Within the family his activity is channelled into conventionally defined roles and in the husband/wife relationship she expects him to dominate.

The husband sees it as his main duty to provide for a secure and happy home. Within the family arena he will have set times or types of activities with the children, particular duties (buying the drinks, servicing the car, house maintenance) and some mini-arenas (the vegetable garden, the garage) which are clearly his and not hers. She will often manage the joint social network. These couples tend to have three social networks, his, hers and a joint one, which is occasionally confined to relations. His network meets outside the home, at work or at the golf club. Hers is around the home and neighbourhood.

These couples run a regulated home. There are routines and rules, tidy rooms and disciplined children. There are usually separate activities pre-scribed for separate rooms, a dining-room, a sitting-room and a kitchen for instance, and if there is space, a study for him which may not often be used. Conversations within the relationship are more often ritual ('how was the office today?') or logistic ('when is your mother arriving?') than issue-raising ('what do you think of the new common market ruling on immigrant labour?'). But whilst there are few deep discussions there are few conflicts. These couples move *away* from each other under tension. The B-type man will channel his tension into a physical ritual. Since there is no appropriate ritual within the home he will take it outside – to sport, the garden or back to his work. The D-type wife tends not to want to express her tensions, protecting the family from them, and suffers in silence and solitude. Tension is not talked out, since their conversation rituals do not allow for it and the norms of the relationship prescribe harmony.

These relationships have a secure predictability based on *traditional* norms. They can appear conventional, even dull, to an outsider, but a man who is fully involved in a work arena may feel that he wants this kind of home base.

In our sample this pattern was not found among the working couples. The reasons are perhaps obvious, but the implications are interesting.

Pattern 2 B–B The pairing of two thrusters

In this pattern both partners place high value on Achievement and Dominance. They *both* want an arena where they can hold responsibility and can demonstrate that they have achieved something. For the husband the arena is most obviously and frequently his work. If, however, he fails to find full satisfaction for those needs in that arena he may turn to another – his family, a hobby, the community. The wife has comparable needs, again most appropriately met by a work arena. In our sample only one of the wives had a full-time, full-commitment job and she was about to give it up as her first baby was due. Part-time work or courses of study were found to be inadequate substitutes by these women. Dominant people need other people. The solitary pursuits of the self-employed or the learner were not, therefore, fully satisfying.

Fully working couples are of course possible within this pattern, even with families and homes to run. But, as the Rapoports pointed out in their study of dual-career families,[2] a high degree of planning and organization is then needed to cope with the logistic and support problems. Thrusting people, however, score low on the dimension 'order' in the EPPS – that is something they prefer to have done for them, preferably by a Caring partner.

The B–B marriages can, therefore, generate considerable discontent. The wife, if children arrive, may find inadequate outlets for her Achievement and Dominance needs in the arena of the family and the marriage relationship. This puts, perhaps, unwanted pressure on both, and may create an atmosphere of competition within the home. If both husband and wife are engaged in their independent work arenas the domestic base may become disorganized, even chaotic. Both may find this irritating. If the husband seeks to blame the wife, wishing on her a 'caring' role, conflict may well develop when she refuses that role. Since Thrusting people can become aggressive under tension, the individuals move *against* each other when they feel tension, clashing in recriminatory arguments.

These, then, are turbulent relationships which have more chance of survival if there are equal opportunities outside the home. They can then concentrate on developing companionship and mutual stimulation. This is a pattern frequently encountered among young marrieds, particularly if they meet while at a college or course, both having strong interests which stimulate one another. It may not easily survive the subsequent stages of child bearing and child rearing unless they evolve a radical innovative pattern, such as sharing the tasks, because the older pattern of support for such a couple (i.e. domestic servants and nannies) is no longer widely available.

We had some suggestions of role separation as one solution, where both partners find quite separate activities for themselves within the family, and conflict is avoided by not meeting. One couple so arranged their lives, apparently without deliberately meaning to, so that they were very seldom in the house at the same time and had no shared networks. They nevertheless saw their marriage as stable and contented.

Pattern 3 A–A The partnership of two 'involved' people

A–A marriages, like B–B marriages, are relationships where two very similar individuals are paired. In our sample A–A and B–B couples had typically met at university, were of the same age and shared similar aspirations, but often had dissimilar family backgrounds. This is in contrast to the 'traditional' B–D marriages where the husband was usually older than the wife, had more years of formal education but came from a similar family background.

The 'Involved' people also are dominant and high-achievers, but these attitudes are tempered, or, more often, confused, by the high value they place on 'caring' and 'belonging'. They prefer to share arenas, not separate them. Their marriages are, therefore, very role-overlapping. There are few clear duties. Whoever is available or enjoys it may cook the meal, clean the house, put the children to bed. People tend to get higher priority than things. Housework and home-maintenance come low on the list. Rooms get used for multiple purposes, and usually reflect it in their decor. Children tend to be full members of the family and can appear 'precocious' or 'undisciplined' to, for instance, a B–D family. Conversations are about issues and values as much as logistics and ritual. Social networks tend to be shared, and therefore often quite small. Tension is high in these marriages, partly because both partners are sensitive, partly because traditional guidelines are not used as prescriptions for behaviour. Under tension both partners first withdraw then move *towards* each other, often talking things out for long hours. These are very intense relationships with the potential for a lot of mutual support.

Both the examples of A–A patterns in our sample could be described as working couples. In each case, however, the wife had young children and only a part-time job. In both cases the husband had a very demanding job and suffered from high tension and stress. Both wives felt that they themselves were under-achieving in their work arenas, but were prepared to tolerate this temporarily in order to support their husband and care for their children. In other words the high value they place on the 'caring' and 'belonging' increased their tolerance for a situation which is antithetical to their needs and values to some extent, and which a more 'thrusting' wife would have resented or rejected entirely.

Pattern 4 A–D An 'involved' husband with a 'caring' wife

The A–D marriage is a version of the A–A partnership which goes less against the social grain. The husband is ambitious for power and achievement but also values 'caring' and 'belonging'. If he is competent he is likely to be working very hard and to be feeling under a considerable amount of stress. His wife, however, will be more willing to support, comfort and protect him than the more egalitarian 'involved' wife, and certainly more than the thrusting wife.

Whilst it is clear that his work is accepted as the most important thing, and her priority is accepted as supportive, the roles are less clear-cut than the conventional (B–D) couple – because the husband *is* so involved and caring. At the same time their lives are less predictable and the tensions less well contained. These relationships are more intense and emotional. There is more questioning and more effort to re-work roles than in the traditional marriages. At the same time there is less competitiveness than in the more involved couples.

Where the wife worked in these marriages it was always a part-time job, but undertaken with a more explicitly multiple motivation to earn money and to provide companionship for herself. The husbands in these patterns often worked far more intensely and for longer hours than their B-type colleagues, not so much because of ambition, but because of the nature of their involvements at work. As a result the home, for their wives, could be a lonely place. In one instance the wife worked as a support to her husband in his work – it was seen to be done to support him rather than for herself.

Working couples were not represented in the other patterns in our series, although theoretically they may be frequently found in the C–C pattern (two existentialists). Two students, for instance, or two artists – people engaged in solitary uncompetitive activities might adopt this kind of relationship where two loners contract, as it were, to each use a common domestic scene, but with little interaction. It is a relationship which may look bleak to others but may seem comfortable to those involved, since it makes little demands on them. Roles are shared out, for convenience; there is little tension; planning minimizes the need to take decisions, get involved in contact, or waste energy in relationships. Many might think it the ideal pattern for working couples. But, while it places few demands on the intimate relationship, it provides few rewards.

Possible scenarios for the future

The evidence of this study is that the working-couple relationship is infrequent and difficult when the husband is a career executive in his mid-30s. In contemporary Britain, this is a situation to which most wives accommodate, some resentfully, and still fewer reject in favour of developing a working-couple pattern. What are the possible scenarios for the future?

One view holds that the 'traditional' relationship in which the bread-winning husband supports the wife who rears the children and minds the home is the natural one and ought to prevail amongst all normal and reasoned people. Another view, the 'modified' conventional one, holds that this pattern should prevail *at a certain stage in life* when there are children and when the husband is under strain in establishing his career. According to this view the problems may come if the couple gets *fixed* in this pattern. A third view finds the conventional pattern inequitable if the wife wishes to work. This position requires the husband and/or his employers to take the necessary steps to facilitate a working-couple pattern. Many marriages nowadays are accommodating to the 'modified conventional model', more through a sequence of stages. An A–A relationship at school or college formed for mutual interests and collegial stimulation may change to a B–B partnership of thrusters as each seeks for dominance in work or career. Then children, particularly nowadays the wished-for children, allow or push one partner (usually, but not necessarily, the wife) into the D quadrant, turning the relationship into a 'traditional' B–D one. As the children grow the D partner often seeks to return to quadrant B and seek self-expression and development in the more aggressive manner of the workplace. With middle-age both partners may move towards an A–A marriage again, rekindling perhaps the mutual interests and under-standings of their early years together. Alternatively, as the family grows up and grows apart a gradual separation of interests can lead to an existential partnership (C–C), an undemanding relationship, separate as each pursues his and her interests in an amicable, or not so amicable, way. This state is sometimes the prelude to a separation or divorce, particularly if one of the partners begins to feel the need to care or be cared for, and seeks a new partner. Alternatively, if the workplace provides a more 'caring' environment rather than an aggressive competition it can be a new job that provides the companionship.

The process of adapting marriage patterns to the requirements and circumstances of our life-cycles can be helped along by conscious thought and understanding. We are not totally the creatures of circumstance. Roles and organizations do shape attitudes and behaviour but the reverse is also true. If we decide that, for a time, the A–D pattern is appropriate for us, we can take steps to bring it into being for ourselves. One couple, once they realised that their conflicts and traumas were the almost inevitable result of their attempt to operate a B–A marriage pattern (he was a thruster and she continued a heavy work involvement as well as having children), turned themselves, within months, into an A–D marriage (it involved his changing jobs, her relinquishing hers). This was acceptable only on the understanding that this would become an A–A partnership once the children were a little older. This has, in fact, occurred.

That was not the only possible solution. A more radical solution would have been for them to consider the restructuring of their occupational roles. Those who feel that this is too difficult to achieve on an individual or couple basis, argue in favour of organizations, or even society as a whole, restructuring the way work is done. These more radical scenarios for the future are described elsewhere in this volume.

Other solutions might involve the couple choosing to remain childless so that they can continue to work; the couple choosing to give less emphasis to performance and success (i.e. setting ambitions lower so as to give more to domestic as well as occupational roles); and the couple arranging participation in group, organizational or state supports for their existing pattern.

Immediate issues

In a business school environment where the sample was taken, most of the people involved are conventional in their attitudes, and most of the organizations who serve as sponsors and employers are unlikely to entertain the more radical solutions except under duress (which may or may not be in times of economic difficulty). Most of the forces, therefore, press young couples into conventional patterns.

For those of them who seek it the concept of working couples becomes a viable one only by accepting the idea of a sequence of marriage patterns. From a more egalitarian early stage, couples in this type of 'greedy occupation' situation can minimize strain by moving to a conventional position while their children are young, then moving back toward one or another of the more symmetrical patterns.

Paradoxically, the business couple in adopting this set of strategic plans for a life-cycle of career-family interplay, may have to accept the fact that they could be going against the new modern norms (especially where the wife is highly educated and trained as well as the husband), against social trends (where more women now work than do not, even when they have children), and perhaps against the norms of their professional friends and associates. If they do this it will be to attain some of the rewards they seek even if they sacrifice, temporarily, others. They seek the maximization of the husband's career (in which the wife shares vicariously and indirectly), the provision of a caring atmosphere in the home by the wife attending to the husband's needs for nurturance and the acceptance by the wife of the benefits of being supported and provided for in order to achieve the satisfactions of mothering, wifely care, and homemaking, during the 'caring' phase.

Though this set of conditions did not require either rationalization or psychological support in the past, it may do so in future for those who choose it. The husband will have to take such steps as are necessary to avoid a pattern of feeling wasted and failing to develop as a person by becoming too engrossed in home-making. These are the new pitfalls of the conventional patterns which are now recognized as real and normal rather than scoffed at as *deviant* or neurotic.

Notes

1 P. Berger and C. Handy, 'Work and family,' unpublished report, London Business School (1974).
2 R. Rapoport and R. N. Rapoport, *Dual-Career Families*, Penguin, Harmondsworth (1971) (out of print). Second edition: *Dual-Career Families Re-Examined*, 1976, London: Martin Robertson; New York: Harper & Row.

3

Hidden and Open Contracts in Marriage

Dan Gowler and Karen Legge

The notion of contract is inseparable from any discussion of marriage, for marriage itself is defined in such terms. At its simplest, it constitutes an agreement between the potential husband and wife that their status of living together should be legally recognized in a way that provides both parties with some mutual rights and obligations towards each other and over the material outcomes of their cohabitation (i.e. children and property). As a contract, it exists until legally dissolved, either by death, or by mutual consent, or by one of the parties behaving in such a way as to be deemed in law to have broken the terms of the contract. Stated like this, marriage itself might appear to be the epitome of an explicit contract. In practice, its apparently clear definition becomes fuzzy on examination.

First, the precise nature of the agreement between the parties, being expressed in only general terms at the outset of marriage (e.g. the husband has the obligation to maintain his wife) is subject to continuous negotiation and interpretation throughout marriage. Yet such an open-ended contract is fraught with hazards. Indeed English law recognizes, through the doctrine of frustration, that circumstances alter and, indeed, may remove a contractual obligation. This being so, it has also to recognize that although the act of marriage constitutes a contract (which if broken by one party, carries financial penalties and obligations), the on-going informal agreements within marriage cannot practicably be legally enforceable (Chitty, 1968). While the law may state that a husband has the obligation to maintain his wife, it has no rights to enforce his *informal* agreement to give his wife a certain sum of housekeeping, nor to force him to pass on the cost of living increases he receives, even if his failure to do so is leaving his family without adequate income for basic necessities. Even where *formal* legal agreements exist about one partner's obligation to the other, and the right of enforcement lies with the courts, the outcome is by no means straightforward. A court can order a divorced husband to provide maintenance for his wife and children, but in practice it can do little if he falls into arrears, as most sanctions it could exercise would only serve to exacerbate the situation. It is small wonder then that the law prefers to leave a family to sort out for itself the reality of its mutual contractual obligations, and shuns intervention even where, as in cases of domestic violence, there might appear good cause for such action.

But if this apparently clear and explicit contract becomes blurred in practice, this is partly because it has to co-exist with and adapt to other contracts or quasi-contracts that the husband and wife have to sustain with other parties. They are likely, for example, to have both formal contractual obligations and informal agreements with a work organization that impinge directly on how they can operate their marriage contract. It is in the balancing and reconciliation of the sometimes conflicting claims that arise from these different sets of obligations that 'hidden' or implicit contracts arise between husband and wife that both influence and are influenced by the way in which the more overt contracts operate. We shall concentrate our analysis, which is based on discussions and seminars with British men and women attending senior management courses, on the hidden or covert contracts.

Work and family arenas

In pre-industrial society, as the family unit was both the unit of production and consumption, work activities and family life tended to be physically integrated, even if highly differentiated by role. In a sense, family life and working life were one and the same thing, differentiation in work-roles being based on, and mirroring that existing in, familial roles (Young and Willmott, 1973). Hence, work contracts tended not to exist as such but to be subsumed under family obligation. In early industrial society, while high levels of role segregation survived in the domestic situation, both in consumption patterns and the (house) work activities carried on there, major income earning activities and family life became physically separated, with the growth of large-scale enterprise and a complex division of labour. Work contracts now became separate from family obligation, but their impact on family relationships was mediated by the conjugal role segregation that still prevailed in the home. Thus, for example, the pattern and number of hours the husband worked had a limited impact on the rest of his family's activities as the family sphere was his wife's responsibility and it was customary for his leisure time to be spent apart from them.

In recent years this situation has changed. Role segregation in the domestic situation has to some extent broken down. Married couples, partly through increased geographical mobility, with separation from kin and long-standing social networks, and partly through changes in social values, have recognized that they are more dependent upon each other. They show a greater willingness to share both the domestic production (housework) and consumption activities (Bott, 1957, cf. Whitehead, 1976). At the same time the husband's occupational role may have become still more remote from the home, as in a white-collar or managerial job he may typically work at activities difficult to define or describe. Even the organization in which he works may have little felt presence in his local community (compare, for example, docking and mining local communities with the 'commuter belt' of metropolitan suburbs). In these circumstances, the relationship between the demands imposed by the husband's work contract and his familial obligations become even less clear, and the potential for conflict may increase. To the extent that such families value mutually shared activities, the demands of the firm, directly affecting the husband's availability, will influence the whole family's ability to pursue this pattern of family life.

The relationship between work and marriage contracts becomes even more problematic when both partners are employed outside the home. If they value 'jointness' in their conjugal relationship, the problems of fitting this into two, rather than one set of external commitments are correspondingly greater. This situation may become particularly acute if the work contracts of both partners assume primary involvement in careers, with the high levels of work commitment that this implies (Wilensky, 1960). One stimulus to making explicit the potentially conflicting demands of work and marital obligations is seen in the development of the 'dual-career family' situation (Rapoports, 1971, 1976; Holmstrom, 1972). Paradoxically, this is *because* this situation is one of the most difficult to manage.

This point will be clarified in the following discussion of the various forms of 'hidden' contract that mediate between work and family obligations in those marital situations, outlined above, that predominate in present day society. That is, the 'conventional' marriage (highly differentiated productive roles – husband at work, wife at home – but some sharing of leisure/consumption activities), the 'working-couple' marriage (less differentiated productive roles – both husband as primary wage-earner and wife as secondary wage-earner work outside the home, although the wife also 'works' at home, and some sharing of leisure/consumption roles), and the 'dual-career' marriage (little differentiation in productive roles in the sense that both husband and wife have similar high levels of commitment to their jobs outside the home, and are both likely to be involved in domestic work within the home, sharing of leisure/consumption roles).

Contracts in the 'conventional' marriage

The conventional marriage may be said to exist, when, to use Bailyn's (1970) terminology, the husband derives his greatest satisfaction from his job/career outside the home, while the wife derives hers, not from a job/ career commitment, but from her activities within the home itself. In other words, a conventional marriage is one in which the career-centred husband with his home-centred wife, engage in a high level of differentiation in their productive roles. Berger and Handy (1975) have similarly characterized this type of marriage as one in which, amongst managers at least, the husband is ideally seen as 'thrusting' (high on achievement/dominance needs, low on affiliation/nurturance needs) and the wife as 'caring', i.e. low on achievement/dominance needs and high on affiliation/nurturance needs. It is this type of relationship that still tends to be seen as the ideal in conventional couples, though it is under increasing pressure from alternative patterns and life-styles.

Such a marriage pattern arises out of and is sustained by an occupational system which in practice if not in theory generally excludes women from most high-status jobs, often justifying this exclusion on the grounds of their higher emotional investment in the family and hence supposedly lower occupational commitment (Safilios-Rothschild, 1976). This is a classical self-fulfilling prophecy (Coser, 1974, p. 90). Excluded from fulfilling work, and having instead sought fulfilment through their families, women cannot then repudiate their sunk investment. 'Thus, not only are women taught and expected to invest their emotions in the family, this investment once more strengthens their attachment' (p. 91).

This being so, the demands of the husband's work-role are generally given a high priority by his wife, as the whole family's position and life-style are seen to be heavily dependent on his success in the occupational system. If the work-role equals a career, the demands on the husband, and their repercussions on his wife, are likely to be immense. For example, career 'commitment' may imply not only a long training prior to full entry into an occupation, but recurrent training and study, often outside office hours; a willingness to take work home, a readiness to travel on work assignments, and to move home, possibly in return for promotion to more demanding if materially more rewarding jobs. Further, the wife may have to accept that her husband's career may become the focus of his interest and aspirations – the arena in which he chooses to establish and develop his 'real' identity.

If the husband desires and accepts a career on these terms, his resulting formal and informal work contracts are likely to rest on the assumption or hidden 'work' contract that his wife will provide the sort of back-up services that are often not just desirable, but necessary if he is to meet the physical, intellectual and emotional demands of his job. The typical manager expects to find awaiting him a supportive, well-ordered domestic scene, where he can find rest and refreshment rather than another set of work demands (Pahl and Pahl, 1971; Young and Willmott, 1973; Berger and Handy, 1975).

Not only do organizations tend to assume that the wives of their career-committed employees will provide a flexible and supportive domestic environment (the converse, in the organization's terminology, being referred to as an employee's 'domestic problems') but frequently also assume that they will give explicitly work-related services, such as the entertaining of the organization's customers or guests; appearance at the appropriate range of social functions and so on. This further expression of the hidden work contract between husband, wife and employer, has been referred to by Papanek (1973) as the 'two person single career', defined as that 'combination of formal and informal institutional demands, which is placed on both members of a married couple, of whom only the man is employed by the institution'. Such demands as they relate to the wife assume the conventional marriage pattern, as they imply that alternative uses of the wife's time are unimportant and unproductive and that the opportunity costs (of external employment, training, etc.) are therefore low. Many companies, for example, will pay toward the costs of a 'hired maid' for company entertainment, but not towards the wife's time. This form of the hidden contract can exist even where there is an explicit ideology of equality between the sexes, which potentially conflicts with implicit (often illegal) inequality of occupational access. It is particularly powerful where the employing organization operates in a social enclave in which it provides the main set of norms for behaviour (e.g. company towns, overseas diplomatic missions, army posts). Moreover, it is seen in situations requiring some kind of mobility (is the wife 'suitable' in the sense of being able to maintain a life-style appropriate to her husband's rank (and potential) within the organization or the environment in which he and the company organization operate?). The organization and employee's public image may also provide insight into these hidden contracts (e.g. the wife may be expected to participate in situations involving various forms of charitable work, in her capacity as the manager's – or minister's – wife).

Sometimes this 'hidden' contract becomes fully explicit, when the wives of foreign service staff are obliged to attend orientation courses before an overseas posting (cf. Baker, 1976), or when large organizations run 'wife programs' to make clear what contributions she can make in support of her husband's career with that organization (Whyte, 1956). More usually, though, the expectations contained in the contract – of appropriate supportive activities to the husband's career on the one hand and a satisfactory promotion rate/material rewards on the other – remain implicit, with the sanctions on non-compliance understood rather than spelt out. Wives who do not provide the expected supports are seen as liabilities, nearly as much as if they drink too much or are indiscreet. But while it is perceived necessary to enlist their participation and loyalty, organizations generally prefer to do so implicitly rather than explicitly.

This hidden 'work' contract in the conventional marriage is often balanced by a complementary hidden 'marriage' contract. The wife may go along with the demands of her husband's career in return for a greater say in other areas. She may expect and be given a more equal share in disposing of the material rewards that result from his career progression, more attention in his free time or a greater range of free time and holidays for herself. Her acceptance of the demands of her husband's career is in return for a sharing of the resultant rewards within the family. This arrangement would appear to work best when the couple have some degree of joint participation in their domestic and leisure activities. For example, Bailyn's (1970) evidence suggests that marriage happiness in such couples depends on this overlap to counter their inbuilt separation of interests.

Generally, the hidden contracts existing in 'conventional' marriages would seem to work in a satisfactory way for most of the couples involved and for most of the time. Thus Bailyn (1970) found that between one-half and two-thirds of the 'conventional' marriages in her sample were very satisfactory to both partners, while Berger and Handy (1975) found that the conventional pattern is more likely to be associated with marital happiness among industrial managers than other patterns. However, dissatisfactions with the contracts implicit in such marriages can develop from two main sources: from confusions arising from the *lack of explicit* agreement about the terms involved (which may come to a head when a career crisis is reached) and from re-evaluations stemming from changes in priorities and values as individuals reach different stages in their marriage and in their lives. Although related, each of these points may be considered in turn.

Lack of explicit agreement about the content and relationship between hidden work and marriage contracts may give rise to problems over the allocation of resources, particularly of time and commitment, to work and family respectively. A frequent issue is whether the organization demands 'too much' from the manager. A husband in one of the more 'greedy' professional or managerial careers may consider that bringing work home every night, working weekends in emergencies, being prepared to be geographically mobile on request, is a normal part of the career he desires (Granick, 1972; Young and Willmott, 1973). He may justify this heavy commitment as benefiting his family materially, even though he may be aware that in practice, if not intention, his work leaves him little time or interest in sharing his family's affluence, or that his family might prefer less of his money and more of his time and interest.

Latent stresses over the balancing of priorities and resources in these hidden contracts may become manifest when a career crisis is reached, which may substantially affect one or both contracts and partners. For example, problems may occur over the geographical mobility involved in the husband's career. From the evidence we have, some wives may welcome regular moves: there is the stimulation of meeting new people, seeing new places, having a new house to arrange, and generally breaking the mono- tony associated with the housewife's role (Pahl and Pahl, 1971; Marshall and Cooper, 1976). In addition, as moves are often associated with promo- tion, in the familiar 'spiral' pattern of mobility, there may be an improve- ment in the level of consumption: more money, a better house in a 'nicer' neighbourhood, better educational opportunities for the children, etc. For such wives (and their husbands) a geographical move may, in fact, validate the mutually beneficial operation of the hidden contracts.

However, for a great many wives, a move may be viewed as a highly stressful process. Not only is the husband, in the initial induction into his new job, likely to have to cope with a heavier than usual demand on his time and other resources, but if the move involves promotion, increased responsibilities are likely to make this situation permanent. At the same time, partly because the husband is fully occupied with acclimatizing him- self to a new occupational role, the wife is likely to bear the brunt of selling one house, finding, buying and arranging another, not to mention the settling of children into new play-groups and schools, and generally estab- lishing for the family a new, if loose, social network of acquaintances and contacts (Pahl and Pahl, 1971; Marshall and Cooper, 1976).

This situation may be particularly painful to the wife if she was firmly embedded in the previous community. Not only may the move have in- volved her in severing rewarding contacts in her local community (from which she may have sought to develop her own identity, separate from husband and children) but, if the family had been settled in the community for a number of years, she may have forgotten how, or lost confidence in her ability, to establish and develop new contacts. Whereas for a husband a move may mean promotion, for a wife it may involve the loss of the status and identity she had acquired for herself in a local community, with the prospect of having to re-establish herself from scratch, using her own initiative and skill to develop informal situations.

A move may not only place stresses on each partner independently, but it may threaten the viability of their hidden contracts. While the husband may feel especially in need of a supportive domestic environment, his wife – coping with her own induction problems (and possibly those of their children) – may have neither the time nor inclination to give this support. She may well be seeking support from him, via an increase in their joint participation in domestic tasks as well as in leisure activities. If she feels that she has been pushed into a move, she may feel that he 'owes it to her' to make a special effort in the domestic sphere. A vicious circle of mutual disappointment and alienation may ensue, with serious consequences.

At different stages in their life-, marriage- and career-cycles, changes in a couples' priorities may occur, changes which have also been documented as a potential source of threat to the maintenance of hidden contracts.

Fogarty *et al.* (1971) and the Rapoports (1975) found that interest in the areas of work, family and leisure tend to shift over time. As children become increasingly independent, and as the husband's career tends to level off (or accelerate yet faster) couples tend to re-examine both the working and relevance of their hidden contracts. The Pahls (1971) found in their sample that a substantial number of wives who accepted the conventional hidden contract early in their marriage, felt disquieted, at midlife, that they had little personal identity, apart from husband and rapidly departing children. It was expressed in such remarks as: 'One of my problems in life is that *i* don't have any idea of what sort of person I am' (p. 112); 'I've been married for twenty-three years now, during which time my husband's wishes, the house and . . . my daughter have always come first and I feel now that I want a life of my own' (p. 216).

While some wives may wish to develop their own identities in an occupational role outside the home at this stage, some husbands may wish to change their occupation or type of work commitment. As Handy (1978) has put it:

> From the husband's point of view, the day when his children leave home can signal the end of his twenty years of obligation. If this moment coincides with a plateau in his career, or a time of sudden disinterest in his accustomed work, it can release a surge of experimentalism. There are plenty of recorded stories of husbands physically leaving home at this period of release from obligation to make us suspect that there must be many more who long for release from the (occupationally) thrusting role that obligations and youth's ambitions thrust upon them. In terms of attitudes and values this release can mean . . . a wish to do one's own thing without ambition or involvement or the desire to dominate.

Whether the nature of these implicit contracts are called into question through a change in one or other partners' priorities, or through a crisis that calls into the open what has previously been implicit, hidden contracts often become open or explicit. In these circumstances the question is raised, whether these contracts should be made explicit from the outset. Before considering this question, however, it is necessary to look at the marriage patterns of 'working couples' in general and the 'dual-career' family in particular.

Contracts between 'working couples'

The 'working-couple' marriage pattern may be said to exist when both partners to the marriage engage in paid employment. Most husbands work full-time, possibly engaging in overtime and shiftworking as well. Wives, in contrast, are much less likely to do so under current conditions, particularly if they have pre-school children.

Nevertheless, the 'working-couple' marriage pattern contains many variants. For example, a career-committed husband may be married to a wife working part-time in a job to which she has little commitment; alternatively both spouses may work full-time in jobs to which they possess a moderate commitment; in some cases the wife's commitment to her work, and her hours spent at work, are greater than those of her husband; in some cases, both may agree to work part-time, in order to achieve what they perceive to be an optimal style of family life as Gronseth (1975) has noted. In a sense, then, variants on this marriage pattern represent a continuum or bridge between that of the 'conventional' and the 'dual-career' marriage. Toward the conventional end the wife's part-time work is an extension of her supportive function ('I just work to provide the family with a few luxuries'), and she sees her external work-role as being clearly subordinated to her home-centred one, and both subordinated to the demands of her husband's work-role. At the other extreme, both husband's and wife's commitment to their respective jobs outside the home, even if they are not careers, may begin to approach that found in the 'dual-career' marriage pattern (see p. 54).

This being so the nature of the hidden contracts between working couples tends to contain elements typical of both 'conventional' and 'dual-career' marriages. Szalai (1972), Young and Willmott (1973), Boulding (1976) and others report that working wives, even if unable to provide the more specifically work-related services that Papanek (1973) itemizes, still undertake the bulk of the housework even if their husbands help out a bit, especially when their wives work full-time. But, although there are some signs of movement towards a breakdown of occupational role segregation in the home, it is not commensurate with the gap created by the wife going out to work. Some research suggests that the increase in male participation in domestic work when their wives also work, is initially confined to 'masculine' activities (e.g. gardening, decorating, DIY, etc.) (Blood and Wolfe, 1960), and Oakley (1974) reports a more disturbing aspect of this tendency. When husbands did participate in the more 'female' tasks, in her London sample, it was almost exclusively in the more enjoyable ones (e.g. playing with children rather than getting up at night to tend them) and that helping with domestic tasks did not extend to accepting major household responsibility. The fact that a wife works, in a secondary way, lends reinforcement to the implicit marriage contract, with joint participation in enriched consumption/leisure activities, warding off any serious consideration about restructuring relationships in their work arenas. It may even strengthen conventional sex-segregated patterns as Meissner *et al.* (1975) have reported in a Canadian study and Aldous (1969) in an analysis of some black American patterns. Thus husbands may withdraw from domestic involvement as strains increase at home, due to the working wife's overload. Insecure husbands may become less involved in the home as their working wives, being less economically dependent on them, are less prepared to 'overlook their personal shortcomings and reward any concern [they] show for the family'. Conversely, if a working wife feels that she is being selfish by working outside the home, feels guilty that she is 'neglecting' her family, she may try to compensate by using potential leisure time for domestic productive activities, and hence maintain, if not reinforce, a conventional pattern. Such evidence as we have would suggest that it is only as the working wife's commitment to her job starts to equal if not surpass that of her husband – as indeed one moves toward the 'dual-career' marriage pattern – that the hidden contracts in work and marriage found in 'conventional' marriage come under sufficient strain to require restructuring, as their implicit asymmetry cannot practicably be maintained (Safilios-Rothschild, 1970).

A 'dual-career' marriage is one in which both husband and wife possess a high degree of commitment to a career (Rapoport and Rapoport, 1971, 1976). Their family commitment may vary (Bailyn, 1970; Handy, 1978).

For such couples, the basic ingredient of the hidden contract in conventional marriage can no longer be assumed. The husband cannot assume his wife's automatic commitment to providing domestic back-up support for his career, any more than can the wife make this assumption about her husband. Yet, for each partner, many decisions affecting his or her career (e.g. about promotion involving geographical mobility, or a heavier commitment in time and other resources) repercuss on that of the other. In contrast to conventional marriages, there can be no assumption that their work activities will be complementary, and as such generate slack resources. Hence the emphasis in their work/marriage contracts shifts away from concern about *boundaries* in allocating the couples' respective resources (and, especially, slack resources) towards an awareness of the interdependent *nature* of their commitments. For this type of marriage pattern to be maintained at all, it cannot rely on implicit understandings to complement conventional ground rules. The assumptions behind the husband's and wife's work and family commitments, and the rules for organizing patterns to implement them must, to be workable, become explicit.

For example, in the case-studies provided by the Rapoports (1971, 1976) it would seem that where the 'dual-career' marriage pattern functioned successfully, the couples had worked out relatively explicit ground rules about how the demands of their respective careers should be reconciled (e.g. neither partners should accept promotion involving geographical mobility if appropriate job opportunities did not exist in that area for the other partner, partners should seek to mutually optimize rather than individually maximize on career potential), how domestic support services should be maintained (which tasks should be undertaken by substitute help, on what basis husband and wife should allocate the remaining tasks) and what kind of family life they desired. But societal pressures, combined with the difficulty of uprooting the conventional 'maps in the head' implanted in early socialization, tend to reassert conventional models under stress, despite preferences for more equalitarian patterns (Rapoport and Rapoport, 1976).

Holmstrom (1972), for example, found that even where there was considerable sharing of household, gardening and child-rearing tasks, 'the ideology of male superiority was prevalent'. Thus the career of the wife was generally given less weight than that of her husband in choice of geographic residence, wives gave up permanent jobs with no secure new job offer when their husbands changed employment (Marceau, 1976), they stepped back when anti-nepotism rules were imposed, and when applying with their husbands for new employment, accepted 'not quite full-time employment or soft money positions, while their husbands were offered full-time firm university contracts'. Similarly, Epstein (1971) found that amongst couples working together in legal practices, wives were given the 'less visible and less prestigious work' along with the practice's non-legal administrative 'housekeeping' tasks (p. 553). Moreover, Rosen *et al.*'s study (1975) shows how external pressures support this reversion to conventional patterns. Discriminatory managerial practices assume that the wife's commitment to her professional obligations will always be secondary to her family ones, and that 'much less support and sacrifice [can be] expected from the husband of a female employee than from the wife of a male employee in similar circumstances' (p. 572). Even in the home, where couples may genuinely seek to move away from such sex-role stereotypes, the Rapoports (1976) report

that it is the wife who must remember about things that have to be done in the home, even though they may have negotiated an agreement to share responsibilities. The husband simply forgets once he has left the house, wiping his mind clean of domestic concerns because he has been programmed by society to shift his attention to external concerns. (p. 368)

One of the reasons that the ground rules of dual-career couples need to be spelled out is *because* western ideologies and structures offer relatively little support for the pattern, even in settings like 'egalitarian' communes, where one might have expected such support (Abrams and McCulloch, 1976). When a marriage pattern is at odds with the prevailing 'custom and practice' (to use industrial relations terminology) it cannot rely on implicit contracts to be supported and supplemented by understandings and case law which are likely to be both irrelevant and/or inappropriate.

Explicit contracts: negotiation and formulation

Along with other commentators (e.g. Sussman, 1975; Weitzman, 1974) we
would argue then that a strong case exists to make explicit the 'hidden'
contracts in marriage. Even in 'conventional' marriages where 'implicit'
understandings, supported as they are by structural (the complementarity
rather than competitiveness of the couple's productive roles) and ideological factors (the belief in male superiority), are most viable, the movement of the partners into a new stage of family/career involvement is
likely to give rise to a need to make explicit what was previously implicit
for purposes of reappraisal and reformation. In marriages where these
supports do not exist, where both husband and wife have the problem of
matching competitive productive roles, in a social context where the
ideology of male superiority is either not accepted or coming increasingly
into question, the contracts between the couple and with the external
organizations in which they work, both need to be, and may be more
acceptable to the parties involved if they become explicit and therefore
negotiable. Yet on what basis might it be suggested that this process is
carried out?

First, the contracts involved may be represented as in Figure 3, in which
the unbroken lines represent explicit contracts, and the broken lines those
which at present tend to be implicit rather than explicit. Arguably, the
marriage contract between husband and wife in a 'dual-career' marriage
may sometimes remain implicit too, but for the reasons suggested above
we consider that the successful working of this marriage pattern can be
increased by making explicit many of the assumptions, expectations and
commitments each partner holds, so that the pressures from role overload
will be contained without retreat into a more conventional marriage
pattern on the one hand, or its dissolution on the other.

We suggest that in making explicit these hidden contracts three inter-
related elements should be taken into consideration: *content*, *style* and
awareness. First, the substantive issues submerged in these contracts need
to be brought into the open through a negotiating framework that poses
two questions: what mutual rights and obligations (in relation to a specific
issue) do both partners think they *should* have, what do they feel they *can*
practicably undertake. The practicality as well as the desirability of a
preferred life-style needs to be considered in terms of its cost and benefits
to each partner and to other members of the family, as well as in terms of
the couple's own abilities, quite apart from willingness, to undertake it.
Second, the couple needs to consider that the appropriateness of different
styles of communications, whether direct, or indirect, may be dependent
both on the nature of the issue involved and on each partner's level of
awareness about the other's position on that issue. Thus, whereas on some
issues, e.g. willingness to move with the job, where there may be already

an open awareness on the part of the couple about their respective views and feelings on the matter, direct open communication may be appropriate and possible. On other issues (e.g. the desirability of having children) where only one partner recognizes that the issue may be problematic, an indirect approach may first be necessary, to heighten the other partner's awareness that an accommodation needs to be sought, before full and open communication on the substantive issue can take place. Additionally both partners should recognize that this process of negotiation is not a once and for all exercise, for as they reach different stages in their working and family life, changed circumstances will call for a re-examination of the appropriateness of existing contracts and, in all probability, their reformulation. Ideally this re-examination should occur well before likely contingencies in work or family arenas materialize; a couple should anticipate them, and together work through their implications before the situation is actually upon them.

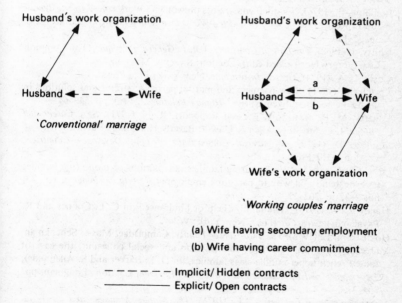

'Conventional' marriage

'Working couples' marriage

(a) Wife having secondary employment
(b) Wife having career commitment

– – – – – Implicit/ Hidden contracts
————— Explicit/ Open contracts

If this process is undertaken, the externally employed partners to a marriage, being more aware of the implications of their own job commitment for the other partner, may be in a better position to judge the extent to which these implications may reasonably be raised and negotiated with the employer. Once these contracts too become explicit, their full implications for the couple can be recognized and a continuing process of revision can be set in motion.

Bibliography

Abrams, P., and McCulloch, A. (1976), 'Men, women, and communes,' in D. L. Barker and S. Allen (eds), *Sexual Divisions and Society: Process and Change*, London: Tavistock.

Aldous, J. (1969), 'Wives' employment status and lower-class men as husbands–fathers: support for the Moynihan thesis,' *Journal of Marriage and the Family*, vol. 31, no. 3.

Bailyn, L. (1970), 'Career and family orientations of husbands and wives in relation to marital happiness,' *Human Relations*, vol. 23, no. 2, pp. 97–113.

Baker, J. C. (1976), 'Company policies and executive wives abroad,' *Industrial Relations*, vol. 15, no. 3, pp. 343–8.

Berger, P., and Handy, C. B. (1975), 'Work and family,' Report of the London Business School, cited in *The Times*, 22 September, p. 16.

Blood, R. O., and Wolfe, D. M. (1960), *Husbands and Wives: The Dynamics of Family Living*, New York: Free Press.

Bott, E. (1957), *Family and Social Network*, London: Tavistock.

Boulding, E. (1976), 'Familial constraints on women's work roles,' in M. Blaxall and B. Reagan (eds), *Women and the Workplace*, University of Chicago Press, pp. 95–117.

Chitty, J. (1968), *The Law of Contracts, Vol. 1: General Principles*, The Common Law Library No. 1 (23rd edn), London: Sweet & Maxwell.

Coser, L. A. (1974), *Greedy Institutions*, New York: Free Press.

Epstein, C. (1971), 'Law partners and marital partners: strains and solutions in the dual-career family enterprise,' *Human Relations*, 24 (6), pp. 549–64.

Fogarty, M. P., Rapoport, R., and Rapoport, R. N. (1971), *Sex, Career and Family*, London: PEP, Allen & Unwin; Beverly Hills: Sage Publications.

Granick, D. (1972), *Managerial Comparisons of Four Developed Countries*, London: MIT Press.

Gronseth, E. (1975), 'Work-sharing families: adaptations of pioneering families with husband and wife in part-time employment,' *Acta Sociologica*, vol. 18, nos 2–3, pp. 202–21.

Handy, C. B. (1978), 'The family: help or hindrance?' in C. L. Cooper and R. Payne (eds), *Stress at Work*, New York: Wiley.

Holmstrom, L. (1972), *The Two-Career Family*, Cambridge, Mass.: Schenkman.

Marceau, J. (1976), 'Marriage, role division and social cohesion: the case of some French upper-middle-class families,' in D. L. Barker and S. Allen (eds), *Dependence and Exploitation in Work and Marriage*, London: Longman, pp. 204–23.

Marshall, J., and Cooper, C. L. (1976), *The Mobile Manager and his Wife*, Bradford: MCB Monographs.

Meissner, M., Humphreys, E., Meis, S., and Scheu, J. (1975), 'No exit for wives: sexual division of labour and the cumulation of household demands,' Mimeograph.

Oakley, A. (1974), *The Sociology of Housework*, London: Martin Robertson.

Pahl, J. M., and Pahl, R. E. (1971), *Managers and Their Wives*, London: Allen Lane.

Papanek, H. (1973), 'Men, women and work: reflections on the two-person career,' *American Journal of Sociology*, vol. 78, no. 4, pp. 857–72.

Rapoport, R., and Rapoport, R. N. (1971), *Dual-Career Families*, Harmondsworth: Penguin.

Rapoport, R., and Rapoport, R. N. (1976), *Dual-Career Families Re-Examined*, London: Martin Robertson; New York: Harper & Row.

Rapoport, R., Rapoport, R. N., with Strelitz, Z. (1975), *Leisure and the Family Cycle*, London: Routledge & Kegan Paul.

Rosen, B., Jerdee, R. H., and Prestwich, T. L. (1975), 'Dual-career marriage adjustment: potential effects of discriminatory managerial attitudes,' *Journal of Marriage and the Family*, vol. 37, no. 3, pp. 565–72.

Safilios-Rothschild, C. (1970), 'The influence of the wife's degree of work commitment upon some aspects of family organization and dynamics,' *Journal of Marriage and the Family*, vol. 32, no. 4, pp. 681–91.

Safilios-Rothschild, C. (1976), 'Dual linkages between the occupational and family systems: a macro sociological analysis,' in M. Blaxall and B. Reagan (eds), *Women and the Workplace*, University of Chicago Press, pp. 51–60.

Sussman, M. B. (1975), 'The four F's of variant family forms and marriage styles,' *The Family Co-ordinator*, October, pp. 563–76.

Szalai, A. (1972), *The Use of Time*, The Hague: Mouton.

Weitzman, L. (1974), 'Legal regulation of marriage: tradition and change,' *California Law Review*, vol. 62, no. 4.

Whitehead, A. (1976), 'Sexual antagonism in Herefordshire,' in D. L. Barker and S. Allen (eds), *Dependence and Exploitation in Work and Marriage*, London: Longman, pp. 169–203.

Whyte, W. H. (1956), *The Organization Man*, New York: Simon & Schuster.

Wilensky, H. L. (1960), 'Work, careers and social integration,' *International Social Science Journal*, vol. 12, no. 4, pp. 543–60.

Young, M., and Willmott, P. (1973), *The Symmetrical Family*, London: Routledge & Kegan Paul.

4

Handling Unconventional Asymmetries

Constantina Safilios-Rothschild and
Marcellinus Dijkers

Status inequality has been the rule in family life in our society. Not only are parents superior to their children in conventional families, but husbands are expected to be superior to their wives – in economic terms, and in education, social status and power. Where asymmetries of this kind are expected there is no problem when they exist. Problems may arise either when the expectations change (e.g. when a wife expects to be *equal* to, rather than inferior to, her husband in family decision-making, etc.) or, when conditions produce unconventional asymmetries, regardless of expectations (e.g. when a wife earns more than her husband, or achieves a higher level of education, though she may not have set out with this as a goal). Both of these forces are at work today, affecting the lives of working couples. In the USA in 1970 over 5 per cent of wives in intact couple families earned more than their husbands, and if one enlarges the basis for comparison to earning 'about the same or more', the proportion rises to about 20 per cent. If one were to broaden the comparison still more and include wives whose jobs had equivalent or higher occupational prestige, regardless of remuneration (as women have often been underpaid for their work), the proportions are still higher according to a study by Lincoln Day (1961). Day observed that this kind of asymmetry did not seem to have a very powerful negative affect on marital satisfaction. This has been accounted for in terms of the fact that in American families the most salient status characteristic is income, so that the preservation of a conventional asymmetry there protects the marriage from being disturbed by unconventional asymmetries in other areas (Safilios-Rothschild, 1976).

A study carried out in Greece provides us with the opportunity to examine the nature and consequences of different types of asymmetries in a very different cultural context than the USA or England. The Greek data are of interest for several reasons. First, there has been much less change in conventional expectations than in America or other advanced industrial nations. Second, the hierarchy of values is different, in the sense that financial success is less supreme as a value, and other values, particularly education, are more important. It may be possible to learn more about the effect of different patterns of unconventional asymmetry – economic, educational, occupational prestige, etc. – on the marriage relationships of working couples.

We studied 250 working women in Athens to examine the effect of status inequalities. We selected couples in different social classes, so that we could attempt to distinguish overall Greek cultural influences from social class influences. We began with the strong impression that education would be a more salient element in the couple relationship than sheer income, because we noted that in many developing countries earning power relates to a variety of factors which do not necessarily reflect the esteem a person is accorded. Education is one of the variables in Greek culture that we expected to be more important than sheer income, or even occupational prestige, in affecting the quality of the husband-wife relationship. And in many Greek families, particularly those in the higher social class groups, earnings do not reflect overall income – much of the real income deriving from a woman's family property, or inherited property, or dowry.

1 Degree of husband's restrictiveness and dominance over the wife

The degree of the husband's restrictiveness or permissiveness was measured on the basis of eight questions tapping the following behaviors which are still often controlled by husbands in traditional Greek contexts: the wife's smoking; wearing lipstick and make-up; going out alone during the day; going out alone at night; talking with neighbors; dancing with other men at parties and weddings; having girlfriends that the husband does not like; and going on summer vacations with the children when the husband cannot come along.

At all levels of wife's education, when the husband is less educated than the wife he is less permissive than when both spouses have the same level of education or the husband has a higher level of education. It is the husband's deficit in education *vis-à-vis* his wife which seems to compel him to become restrictive and to oppress his wife, and this holds true regardless of the husband's particular level of education.

When the wife's level of education is examined separately in relation to permissiveness, we find that the lower the level of education the less permissive the husband. Since there is a considerable educational similarity between spouses, many husbands of women with little education have little education themselves. And there is considerable evidence that Greek men with a low level of education hold traditional sex-role values that include the desirability and even the necessity to control their wives' lives (Safilios-Rothschild, 1967a; 1972). We find, therefore, that the most restrictive and oppressive husbands are those whose wives have a low level of education and who themselves have an even lower education. The wife's educational superiority in this case seems to cause considerable strain that has to be counteracted by the husband who feels inadequate because he cannot live up to the traditional expectation of male superiority.

When we look at income differentials between spouses, we find that in general the larger the wife's contribution to family income as compared to the husband's contribution, the more restrictive is the husband of the wife's activities and behaviors. Finally, the occupational status inequalities between spouses seem to affect permissiveness in the same manner as educational inequalities. Regardless of the occupational level or educational level of the wife, the husband's deficit in occupational status *vis-à-vis* his wife seems to result in his reduced willingness to accept his wife as an autonomous human being. Again, probably partially as a reflection of education, the lower the wife's occupational status (and hence most often also the husband's), the more restrictive the husband.

It seems, therefore, that the educational or occupational superiority of the wife that may lead to her contributing considerably, equally, or more than the husband to the family incomes, tends to make Greek husbands defensive and deficient in terms of stereotypic masculinity. Since they have failed to fulfil the stereotypic expectation of male superiority on the important status dimensions, they revert to a more primitive level of masculinity by 'bossing' around, controlling and restricting their wives in order to reassure themselves of their 'superior' position. Otherwise, they are probably afraid that their wives may feel entitled to dominate them. It seems, therefore, that the status superiority of the wife on any dimension is threatening to the husband and creates considerable tension.

2 The management of money

When two independent incomes are earned in a family, the question as to who has the authority to manage the money becomes crucial and reveals important aspects of the dynamics in the husband-wife relationship. Despite the fact that in the Greek study the question asked directly referred to the management of the wife's income, the answers do in fact provide information about the overall style of money management.

The breakdown of the different styles of money management are as follows:

1　She takes whatever she wants (4%).
2　She asks her husband for whatever she needs (6%).
3　She takes what she needs before turning over the money to her husband (3%).

4   He gives her whatever she needs for personal expenses (4%).
5   His and her money is pooled, each takes whatever he or she needs (27%).
6   She manages the money (22%).
7   They each manage their own money (34%).

It is the less-educated women and the women working in a lower level job who most often give an answer indicating a low or a lack of autonomy in spending the money they have earned (answers 2, 4). But it is also these wives who most often indicate that they manage all the family's money (answer 6). The highest independence of husband and wife in spending, as expressed in answers 5 and 7, is characteristic of those families in which the wife has a high educational and occupational level.

These results are not very surprising – except perhaps for the high percentage of families (34 per cent) in which the husband as well as the wife manage their own money. Again basing our argument on the empirically found correlation between husband's and wife's educational and occupational level, we conclude that it is the husband of low education and occupation who holds his wife on a tight leash when it comes to spending the money she has earned. Most probably they are the husbands who by their income put their wives in a situation where they must work and who hold the traditional viewpoint that a woman should not be trusted with money – or who simply appropriate the wife's income. The pattern that, according to impressions and the research literature, is most common among blue-collar workers in western Europe: the husband turns his money over to his wife, who is the financial manager, is less frequently found in the Athenian sample. Only 41 per cent of the women with a blue-collar job and 30 per cent of the women with a (lower) vocational school or lesser education report this type of money management.

The above conclusions are confirmed when we take into account a characteristic of the husband himself: his income level. The lower the husband's income, the more often we find the pattern that the wife asks for the money she needs, but also the more often she has sole responsibility for managing the family income. The higher the husband's income, the more often we find that each spouse manages his own money.

How is the method of money-management employed by these families influenced by inequalities between husband and wife? The income of the wife relative to that of her husband seems to be of prime importance here. The income inequality has different effects in various income groups (based on the husband's income). At the lower income levels, it holds true that the larger the wife's financial contribution the less often she is manager of the money, while at the two highest income levels, this trend is reversed: here the wife has sole responsibility more often when her income approaches that of her husband. The findings concerning the effects of educational and occupational inequality are similar: for wives at a high occupational or educational level, superiority over the husband earns them the 'right' to manage the money of the entire family. For wives at a low educational and occupational level, in cases of superiority over the husband the trend is reversed: their husbands, probably threatened by their wives' superiority, do not let them have the sole responsibility for money-management.

Completely independent management of the money earned by the husband and the wife is more frequent in the higher educational, occupational and income groups especially, when the husband earns more than the wife or when he has a superior occupational standing than his wife. It seems that when the Greek husband has a securely high social standing in terms of income, education and prestige, and a higher one than his wife, he feels comfortable with his wife having financial autonomy. His high standing reassures him of his 'masculine' achievement so that he does not have to control his wife's money in order to feel the head of the household.

The third most frequently used method of money-management, the pooling of money, shows quite different patterns. The higher the wife's income in comparison with that of her husband, the more often the money is pooled (regardless of the income level of the family). In this case, the wife's income superiority seems to create considerable strain that can be reduced by the pooling of the money, a technique that helps make the available money a common resource, thus erasing the wife's 'right' to the greater portion of this money. The higher the wife's educational or occupational level in comparison with her husband, on the other hand, the less often the money is pooled.

3 Division of labour

One type of strain in the marital relationship could result from wives with higher education, prestige, or income demanding that their husbands shoulder a sizeable share of familial tasks and responsibilities. In the upper and upper-middle class, of course, the availability of a live-in maid usually makes this issue less relevant, although even there someone has to overview, guide and assume the responsibility. In fact in our sample, at the highest income level (the husbands') three-fourths of the families have a maid. The wife's relative financial contribution to the family income is also of considerable importance. At all levels of the husband's income, the higher the wife's income relative to that of her husband, the greater the probability of hiring the services of a maid.

As can be expected, Greek husbands, in general, offer little help in household chores when there is a maid, but it seems that it is the husband's level of education which influences the extent to which he adheres to traditional masculine stereotypes that is a crucial variable in the determination of the type of prevailing division of labor. The higher, in general, the husband's education is, the more 'liberated' he tends to be with regard to participating in household tasks. When, furthermore, wives have as much or higher income than their husbands, low-educated Greek husbands react to this threat by altogether retreating from any participation in family tasks and responsibilities.

From previous research studies there is some evidence that traditional low-educated Greek husbands decide if and when their wives will work (Safilios-Rothschild, 1967b) and as we already saw manage the money she earns (or use it from a common pool). In this way, in traditional Greek working and low-income families, the wife's work and earning power, even when higher than that of the husband, does not become a resource that earns her any 'rights' and is not allowed to create any tensions. The husband remains the 'boss' who, therefore, relegates all housework and familial responsibilities to his wife who is forced to carry a fully double-role burden.

It is almost a paradox that in the case of better-educated men who usually have enough money to hire a maid (and they most often do so), the income superiority of (or equality with) the wife makes them take an active part in the household division of labor. It seems, therefore, that the husband's extent of liberation from stereotypic masculinity not only helps ease the tension that can be produced from the wife's high earning power but it also makes him willing to help share the familial responsibilities even when there is no acute need.

4 Communication between spouses

All couples must communicate at the information-instrumental level about the everyday tasks and routines, if they are to function even at a minimal level. This type of communication, therefore, says little about the nature of the husband-wife relationship. A much more sensitive type of marital communication is the discussion of worries, tensions, problems, feelings and emotions. It can be hypothesized that, in general, in our society, the better the relationship between spouses the greater the degree of such communication. And there is evidence that the higher the spouses' education the greater the overall communication between the two (Safilios-Rothschild and Hector, 1976).

In this area of marital interaction, it seems that the wife's superiority when the woman is very well-educated and has a prestigeful job, strains the communication between spouses. Status similarity between spouses is the most conducive to communication. At an intermediate level, however, of the wife's education and prestige, it is the husband's superiority (but not a too great one) that is the most conducive to this type of marital communication. Finally, when the wife has only an elementary school education such communication is so uncommon that one cannot discern any pattern.

5 The sexual relationship

The better educated Greek women seem to be much more often satisfied with the sexual relationship with their husbands than the less educated. In our sample about 80 per cent of those with at least a high school education were satisfied, while only 50 per cent of those with less education were satisfied. Furthermore, a Greek woman's satisfaction with the sexual relationship, regardless of her level of education or occupation, increases with the educational or occupational superiority of the husband. This finding tends to indicate that Greek women, as expected by traditional sex-roles, are sexually more 'turned on' by their husbands when they consider them their superiors. It is, however, also true that a Greek woman's satisfaction with marital sex increases not only with her own educational and occupational level but also with that of her husband. A supplementary plausible explanation is that the higher the education of the husband the greater the attention he pays to his wife's sexual satisfaction and the more willing he is to use contraceptives (the use of which in Greece is almost entirely up to the men) and thus to alleviate her fears of possible pregnancy.

In the case of wives with a low-level education, they are most often married to men with a low level of education who, as we already saw, hold traditional masculine values. These values make them treat their wives as their sexual property which they can use when they want and as they want, without much concern about their wives' wishes, preferences, degree of satisfaction or willingness to have sex. Evidence from case studies of traditional Greek couples indicates that there is rarely any sexual foreplay and that husbands are not concerned with whether or not their wives have experienced an orgasm (Safilios-Rothschild, 1968). This explains why half of these wives are not satisfied with marital sex; why 12 per cent of them find marital sex boring or disgusting; and why they rarely do dare refuse to have sex whenever their husbands want to, even when they are very tired, in a bad mood, angry with their husbands, or do not want it for any other reason. The sexual relationship brings them little pleasure and is most often imposed upon them as an added unpleasant marital duty. In fact, low-educated women seem to be so much oppressed and dominated by their husbands that even their status superiority in terms of income, occupational prestige, or education does not change the situation. They cannot use their status superiority as a resource to improve their position *vis-à-vis* their husbands. As we saw earlier, low-educated women cannot use their status superiority as a resource in any area of marital interaction examined. It is not, therefore, surprising that the same holds true with respect to marital sex, an area in which any challenge on the part of the wife would be exceptionally threatening to a traditional man. Their own traditional socialization, on the other hand, has prepared them to accept a subordinate position to their husband and to be afraid to challenge him in any way, particularly to refuse him sex, so that he does not abandon them for another woman.

Greek wives, on the contrary, with at least some years of high-school, seem to gain sufficient self-confidence from their status superiority to refuse to have sex with their husbands when for a variety of reasons they do not feel like it. This may also explain why women at a higher level report greater satisfaction with marital sex: having a certain amount of control as to when it takes place, so that they most often have sex when they are in the mood, can do wonders for their satisfaction.

6 Satisfaction with the marital relationship

How satisfied wives are with their marriage is largely a subjective matter considerably influenced by the wives' expectations from marriage which are in turn determined by their sex-role definitions. The more traditional the wife, the less she expects understanding, tenderness or companionship from her husband and the more she tends to be satisfied with her marriage as long as he is a good breadwinner and is not openly unfaithful to her. In trying to cover a wide spectrum of possible expectations that wives may have from their marriage, marital satisfaction was measured with regard to the degree of existing tenderness, understanding, companionship, the standard of living, the sexual relationship and relatively in comparison with other couples.

The effect of status inequalities between spouses on the wives' marital satisfaction varies according to their level of education. Wives with the lowest level of education are more satisfied with their marriage the more education their husband has in comparison with themselves. The best educated women, on the other hand, are the most satisfied when they are about equally well-educated as their husbands or when their husband is more (but not much more) educated than they themselves.

The wife's education is here an important intervening variable because it is highly relevant to the types of values and expectations the wife has from marriage. Low-educated women hold predominantly traditional values and under the influence of sex-role stereotypes expect their husband not to be their equal but their superior. When, therefore, men are their inferior, they feel quite unhappy since they tend to evaluate their husband and their marriage as a failure. Well-educated women, on the other hand, increasingly espouse egalitarian beliefs that allow them to appreciate and enjoy their husbands and their marriage even when they are more educated than their husbands.

Income inequality follows the same pattern as education inequality. Less-educated women are less satisfied with their marriage the greater their contributions to family income in comparison to those made by their husband. Again, the traditional sex-role stereotypes make less-educated women expect to be fully provided for by their husbands and they tend to resent and devaluate their husbands when they themselves have to contribute a considerable part of the family income. Previous studies have shown that when working and low-income women have to work, their decision to work often is imposed on them by their husbands or their actual low standard of life (Safilios-Rothschild, 1967a). In the case of well-educated women, however, the extent of their financial contribution does not influence their satisfaction with the marriage.

It seems, therefore, that status inequalities between spouses are evaluated differently according to the extent to which wives hold traditional sex-role stereotypes. Whether or not status inequalities produce tensions and affect satisfaction from marriage depends not only on the type and degree of status inequality but also on the wife's sex-role values.

The same conclusions are reached when, instead of the overall marital satisfaction, satisfaction with specific aspects of the marital relationship, such as tenderness, understanding, companionship or sex, are examined separately.

Discussion

The Greek data examined in this chapter show that the impact of status inequalities between spouses is very different in different social classes. This is primarily due to the fact that in urban Greece there are great differences in the extent to which traditional sex-role stereotypes influence the thinking and behavior of men and women in different social classes and levels of education. The majority of working and low-income couples living in Athens are usually of rural origin having migrated to the capital during the last decade. They still adhere to traditional sex-role stereotypes according to which the husband must be able to occupy the unchallenged superior position in the family in terms of knowledge, prestige in the world, as well as finances. Within this context, it is clear why the wife's equality to or superiority with regard to any characteristic is very threatening to her husband as well as to herself. Possible tensions resulting from this superiority of the wife that could disturb the marital interaction are not only managed but most probably entirely prevented by the masculine assertion of the husband over his wife. In doing so the husband makes sure that her superiority will not be used by the wife as a 'resource' in order to gain power or independence. In this way her status superiority not only does not improve her position in the family but it often leads to her greater oppression, since her behavior tends to be more controlled and restricted and the money she earns more often managed and controlled by her husband. This pattern can occur because Greek women in this traditional context are socialized to like and respect a domineering, strong man so that they may tend to accept their oppression as a sign of masculine 'superiority'. Traditional men try to make up their status deficit *vis-à-vis* their wives by sheer bossiness and control.

In the case of well-educated couples, on the contrary, the wife's superiority seems to considerably affect the marital interaction so as to earn her 'rights' and to improve her position in the family. This superiority is thus used as a valuable and powerful resource. While there is no indication that these husbands react so as to minimize the effects of their wives' superiority, we cannot be sure whether or not this superiority creates tensions or how such tensions are coped with by the husbands, since only wives were interviewed in this study. It is possible, for example, that well-educated husbands handle their wives' status superiority and the resulting effects upon the marital relationship by not perceiving any such effects.

It is interesting to note that the wife's educational superiority does not seem to have any greater or more special effect on marital interaction than other types of superiority. In fact, it seems that it is the wife's income superiority that may be the most 'touchy', since at all educational levels when the wife earns as much or more money than her husband, it is pooled together so as to lose the 'identification tags'.

Implications

What are the implications of the Greek study for our understanding of how unconventional asymmetries may be handled, in other countries as well as in Greece? First, we note that they are not as different in Greece as we had expected. As in America economic asymmetries are still a very 'touchy' point, despite the fact that there may be differences between the two cultures in the relative evaluation of education, occupational prestige, and so on.

Second, as in America, there are class differences in the ways in which these asymmetries are handled – though we do not have sufficiently detailed information about America to know whether the resemblances in distribution of these asymmetrical patterns exist. In America, many couples in which the wife earns more than the husband are to be found in lower income groups, where the unemployed or sporadically employed male may be more prevalent.

But, regardless of the prevalence within the different class groups, it is useful to consider what it may be about the social classes that makes it more difficult for people in the lower socio-economic occupational groups and the more traditional-minded groups who have come from rural backgrounds to confront and satisfactorily manage unconventional asymmetries. The most obvious point is educational differences. The higher the social class, the higher the educational level, on the whole, and therefore the greater capacity to understand and communicate about different patterns of value and behavior. Given the nature of urban life, in the higher social classes, especially in Greece, more command of resources is available to spouses to arrange supportive services to the family, day-care services, domestic help services, and so on.

We cannot provide any definitive proof for a final assertion that we would like to make, but it seems reasonable from available data and experience to suggest that there is a further factor, an 'X' factor, which allows husbands and wives to tolerate one another's search for self-realization. This factor operates best when there is less economic hardship, and when there is a greater cultivated capacity to communicate and resolve conflicts. But it can operate at all levels, and consists in an *interpersonal* perspective on the relationship, whereby the partners are able to see one another in positive couple terms. This is different from the dependency and vicarious fulfilment of needs that has characterized conventional couple relationships; and it is different from the competitive and rivalrous interactions that sometimes accompanies early efforts at egalitarian couple relationships. This interpersonal perspective is one of mutual respect and friendship, which must be achieved in some way, if the couple is to sustain the working-couple pattern. Economic difficulties can interfere with the task, and as it is not an easy thing, the lack of education and communication skills can also hamper it. But money and education alone do not assure that it will happen. Greek middle-class couples, like their American and European counterparts, work at the process relatively successfully. But it must be remembered that this is still an ongoing process which cannot be achieved automatically. Both spouses have to continuously work hard in order to reach it and sustain it.

Bibliography

Day, L. (1961), 'Status implications of the employment of married women in the U.S.,' *American Journal of Economic Sociology*, 20, December, pp. 390–98.

Safilios-Rothschild, C. (1967a), 'A comparison of power structure and marital satisfaction in urban Greek and French families,' *Journal of Marriage and the Family*, 29, 2, pp. 345–52.

Safilios-Rothschild, C. (1967b), 'Some aspects of fertility in urban Greece,' *World Population Conference, 1965, Vol. II: Fertility, Family Planning and Mortality*, New York: United Nations.

Safilios-Rothschild, C. (1968), 'The dynamics of sexual relationships in traditional Greek families,' unpublished manuscript, Detroit, Michigan.

Safilios-Rothschild, C. (1972), 'The options of Greek men and women,' *Sociological Focus*, 5, 2, winter, pp. 71–83.

Safilios-Rothschild, C. (1976), 'Dual linkages between the occupational and family systems: a macrosociological analysis,' *Signs*, 1, 3, part 2, spring, pp. 51–60.

Safilios-Rothschild, C., and Hector, J. (1976), 'The correlates of marital communication in urban Greece,' unpublished manuscript, Wayne State University.

5

Parenting

Working Family Project

Each year since the Second World War ever-increasing numbers of married women have joined the American labor force. The rate of increase has been even more dramatic for mothers of young children. This trend, now affecting about half of all couples, carries important implications for the organization and management of family life. With many women now spending a sizeable portion of their day away from the home, husbands and wives need to make major readjustments in household and child-care responsibilities. At present, women in American society are normally expected to bear total or near-total responsibility for home and child care. However, as the social anthropologist, Beatrice Whiting (1972), points out, American society is unusual in the value it puts on the mother remaining home with the children all or most of the time.[1] Mothers in most societies are expected to spend four to six hours each day outside the homestead.

Feelings about being a parent are related in part to the values of the outside society. Parents attempt to measure their ability and their satisfaction against a societal yardstick that tells them what they should be doing and how they should be feeling. Thus American dual-worker families find themselves caught between two pressures: on the one hand, powerful cultural expectations, and on the other, the pressing logistical problems of managing their household, child care, and both parents' jobs.

In this article we explore what being a parent means in the families we studied and describe some of the resources available to parents. This includes help families can receive from neighbors, friends, relatives and services for hire, both in the sense of services and of 'psychological resources' such as advice, support and approval. In our research we have looked intensively at fourteen families in which both adults work, to find out what kinds of child-care and household arrangements families make, how they arrive at them, and how they feel about both the decision-process and their decisions. Through interviews and observations we explore how feelings about employment, making a home and being a parent are inter-related. Our presentation of this research moves from a general consideration of the state of parenting at this time in our society to an analysis of the particular situations and processes of adjustment in our sample families.

Our data, then, are a combination of factual information on schedules, assigned responsibilities, social contacts and resources; and of the feelings expressed by both of the parents about their work, home responsibilities, and themselves as spouses and parents. Table 1 introduces you to the fourteen families. These families illustrate a great diversity of approaches to the care of their children and in the feelings they express on child-related issues. In addition, in each of these families there have been similarly diverse efforts to allocate household chores to allow the mother to work outside the home.

TABLE 1   *Families interviewed*

Families	*Husband's occupation*	*Hrs/Wk*	*Wife's occupation*	*Hrs/Wk*	*No. of children*
Deneux	business manager	40	keypunch	35	2
Farlane	salesman	35	nurse	24	5
Henry	maintenance	40	factory	35	2
Hunt	business manager	40	keypunch	25	2
Jackson	factory	40	nurse	24	4
Long	factory	40	secretary	15	2
Nelson	teacher/salesman	65	nurse	15	9
Parks	student	30	day care	15	1
Raymond	business manager	55	saleswoman	20	4
Samuels	armed forces	40	day care	25	2
Sandle	student	40	nurse	40	1
Sedman	maintenance	40	keypunch	25	2
Tilman	draftsman	40	administration	40	1
Wyatt	fireman/ construction	55	secretary	40	2

The families we studied are dual-worker families, but not dual-career families (Rapoport and Rapoport, 1971; Holmstrom, 1972). Almost all the men work full time, and some are occasionally employed in a second job. The women's work-hours range from a few hours per week to full time. Most of the men have been at their present jobs a long time and several reported having traded jobs with greater interest (or the option of seeking them) for their present job with more security – usually around the time of the birth of their first child. The men take their role as provider very seriously.

Though none of the families are in poor economic straits, economic stress is a continual aspect of their daily environment. Many of them attain levels of income near the national median ($10,955 for a family of four according to the 1970 Census) only with the wife's contribution. Thus, her economic role, while perhaps not large in actual amount or even as a fraction of total family income, may be relatively more important to these family's standard of living than is the case for dual-professional families. The extent to which the wife's employment is necessary is often a source of tension and difference of opinion in the families with husbands generally minimizing it and wives making more of it. The need to work for economic reasons is generally more acceptable than the simple desire to work. Implicitly and sometimes explicitly it is sometimes felt that a working wife reflects badly on a man's ability as a provider, yet the families use and enjoy the extra income. Economic stress is also seen in the fact that cost becomes a factor in determining family size – some families report that they decided on fewer children when they realized they could not afford a family of the size they originally intended. This, in turn, increases the wife's capacity to sustain a work role.

Resources for child rearing

Child care

With both parents working, parents, in the families we visited, resort to a wide variety of child-care arrangements. This is partly because day care of good quality is costly and usually difficult to find, and partly because there is considerable variation in what families consider desirable. In each of these families, deciding who, if anyone, they trust to take over the role of substitute parent to their child is an important family issue.

Preferences aside, many of the families are forced to combine a series of alternatives – care by each spouse in turn while the other was at work, hired babysitters, informal child-care exchanges, assistance from relatives if there are some nearby, and formal day care or nursery programs. The complexity of child-care scheduling is often remarkable.

In the Wyatt family, for example, the wife works full time at a nearby real estate agency as a secretary, where she is also studying real estate sales and management. Mr Wyatt is a fireman and works part time as a carpenter. Mrs Wyatt rises at 5.30 each morning of the week to begin readying the children, Christopher, six, and Oliver, four, for school. She finds this easier than getting the children up later and rushing them: then the children balk, and she is later than ever. Chris attends first grade at a neighborhood school; Oliver is in a local nursery school program from nine to twelve, three days a week. A neighbor and friend, whose son attends the same nursery, drives Oliver to school and then picks the boy up at twelve. Mrs Wyatt has to leave by 8.00 a.m. for work, so Chris walks to a friend's house nearby and waits there to go to school with him. When Chris comes home from school at 2.30, he picks up Oliver and the two boys walk to another neighbor's house, and she cares for them until 5.00 p.m., when Mrs Wyatt picks the boys up on her way home from work. On the two days when Oliver does not have school, he usually stays with this babysitter all day.

During the evenings and on weekends, the Wyatts take turns watching the boys, as Mr Wyatt may be working or there are various errands to run. This complicated schedule can be easily undone, as happened recently when the afternoon babysitter's husband became seriously ill. Mrs Wyatt's mother lives in a nearby town and was able to fill in for a few days, until a temporary substitute up the street could be found. Illness and other emergencies are a constant threat to the stability of such arrangements, and when asked what she might change about them, Mrs Wyatt replied, somewhat poignantly, 'I'd just like something a little more permanent – not so many changes.'

The Wyatts use a formal child-care program. Other families don't like the idea of paid outsiders caring for their children or they find paid child care too expensive. In several study families, the parents have arranged their work schedules so that each can be at home to care for the children during the time that the other is working. They make little use of out-of-home care except for occasional child care by near-by relatives or close neighbors. For instance, Mr Long works a shift at a warehouse from 5.00 p.m. until 1.00 a.m. with occasional overtime. He comes home around 2.00 a.m. and sleeps until 9.00 or 10.00. Mrs Long has a part-time job where she is allowed to vary her hours within certain limits. She usually works as a typist from 10.00 a.m. until 2.00 p.m., but occasionally goes to work later if her husband has worked more overtime than usual and is sleeping later. Each of them is responsible for the children while the other is working. One of the results of the arrangement, Mr Long explained, is that he now understands why his wife liked to get away from the house and kids. After he had started caring for the children alone while his wife worked, he was really glad when she returned and took over and he could go to work for some peace and quiet. Parents who adopt this pattern often feel that parents are always the best people to care for young children. The major cost to such parents is that they have little time together with the children and little time alone together.

Some families rely on close neighborhood groups to help with child care. The Henry's provide a good example of this pattern. Though we did not obtain exact information on their child-care pool, it does not currently

involve the exchange of money, though it did at some time in the past.
At least three families on their street are involved, and scheduling and
reciprocity seem very informal. 'Leila takes the Marsh's kids, and mine.
Now I'll watch hers and the Marsh's little boy,' Mrs Henry explains. 'It's
done for nothing – there's no money, it's just a friendly thing. . . . It does
get tiring sometimes. I had five the other day, and I was glad to see them
go.' On our daily log, a record of visits and visitors in the family over a
week's time, Mrs Henry noted that Leila twice left her child for two or
three hours in the mid-morning. Another neighbor, not mentioned in Mrs
Henry's description of the informal arrangement, also left her infant
briefly. The Henry's did not receive any child-care aid during this week,
but Mrs Henry was recovering from an illness and was not working during
this time. However, Leila did come to help Mrs Henry clean her oven,
suggesting that the 'exchange' system may be broader than just child care,
encompassing a range of mutual-aid activities. Before this neighborhood
exchange system developed, the Henry's had hired teenaged babysitters,
and were very dissatisfied with them. They felt these young sitters were not
sufficiently responsible to be left alone with their children and their apart-
ment.

These three families have found very different solutions to the problem
of child care while both parents are employed. Although the families use
a wide variety of arrangements, in the end they all depend primarily on
themselves because of limited resources. The parents must be prepared to
underwrite all services – they are 'on call' all of the time. A breakdown in
some link, such as an illness or a missed ride, can be a disaster, and one
parent or the other must be prepared to give up their plans. All of these
parents have put tremendous care and planning into their arrangements to
make sure their children were well cared for.

In addition to reflecting people's feelings about being parents and their
reaction to general societal values concerning parenting, the use and choice
of child-care programs may also reflect how parents feel about their other
activities. Mrs Wyatt, for instance, feels that she is at the beginning of a
career. She is investing herself in work and study now in preparation for a
better job in the future. Working at a full-time job is important enough to
her to justify the expense of nursery school. For some of the mothers,
although some experience other than housework and child care is sought,
job advancement is not an important goal. Mrs Long, for example, has a
low-paying, part-time clerical job, primarily to get out of the house and
relax from her home and child-related responsibilities. This was also important to Mrs Wyatt, who returned to the labor force when her youngest
was three, and comments: 'I felt like I couldn't carry on a decent conversation with anybody over six years old.' Mrs Henry works longer hours on
an assembly line, seeing her work as a necessary but temporary measure to
help pay for the family's recent purchase of a piece of land.

Several of the families have tried out-of-home child care and met initial resistance from their small children. One difference between the families who stayed with it and those who did not seems to be that in the former the wife sees her job as more than a respite or minor source of extra income and is willing to wait out the period of the child's discontent in the child-care situation. In the latter, the family stops the use of day care after a day or two of the child's complaints. Some families see day care as a positive influence on their children, providing them with experiences and peer contact they would miss by staying at home. The families who relent immediately often do so because the women see in their child's discontent confirmation that their roles as mothers are and should be the primary focus of their lives. So while they continue to work they also shoulder the burden of child care.

Advice and support

What other kinds of help do parents have access to and use? Attitudes and information about parenting come from many sources. All of the parents had at least one first-hand experience of parenting as the children of their own parents. Mothers and fathers in the families usually use their own parents as one of the standards by which to judge their own parenting. However, while some parents hope they can be as good as their own parents, others wish to be different. Mrs Henry, for example, says, 'I only hope I can be as good a mother as mine was,' while Mr Wyatt reports, 'I try to be in every way different from my father. I could never understand how he could be so mean to little kids.' Overall, while parents sometimes seek advice from relatives, there seems to be a consensus that they are not generally helpful sources of advice and suggestions about child-rearing. Mr Henry remarks, 'I don't think the way I raise my children is any of my relatives' business – if their kids were perfect I'd go to them and ask how they did it, but they're far from perfect.'

Resistance to the advice of grandparents often reflects the wish to differentiate or separate the new family from the families in which the parents themselves grew up. This is an important task for all families in our culture, especially in the early years of a marriage. It may be a particularly necessary one where the new parents live in close proximity to their own families of origin, as many in our sample do.

The Sedmans expressed another common sentiment when they say: 'We don't talk to relatives about child rearing much. Times have changed and the problems are different. [The grandparents say] "Oh, my children never did that." But they did something else that you never heard about. . . .' It should be noted, however, that while young parents resist grandparental help in the form of advice on child-rearing practices, they are more receptive to help in the form of physical child care and financial help for major purchases, such as a house.

The sense that 'times have changed' and the wish to establish independence from families of origin seemed to be a major factor in some of the families' heavy reliance on experts. For example, Mrs Wyatt says: 'My mother is really of the old school. . . . She and my friends – they all had different advice. It sort of confused me. I could occasionally call on my sister-in-law, but the doctor was my Rock of Gibraltar. He was great. . . .' Other families express a certain ambivalence about expert opinion, however, even about the ubiquitous Dr Spock. 'When they were sick or something,' Mrs Long remarks, 'I'd look it up. . . . Otherwise, he [Spock] has a lot of screwy ideas.' And Mrs Hunt says: 'When I first started out, I lived with Dr Spock. Then I decided, I'm not going to bring my children up out of a book!'

So the psychological supports for parents, then, are few, and often confusing. Although they confer with relatives, neighbors, friends or experts, most parents we talked to rely heavily on their own inner resources and on talking things over with their spouse. Even though parents may feel they are doing a good job of raising their children even without support and reinforcement that their way is somehow 'right', there may remain a residual doubt. This becomes especially painful when things are not going smoothly and the parents have no reference point from which to evaluate who is responsible for a problem and how to solve it.

One of the consequences of parental uncertainty seems to be that attention is focused on the child to measure the relative success or failure of parental child rearing. The child becomes the 'product' or 'output' of parental 'inputs'. This puts enormous pressures on parents and exacerbates their uncertainty, since a judgment on the success of their finished child 'product' will not be available for fifteen or twenty years. For some parents this pressure results in the belief that only parents can really know and care for their children properly. In addition, they feel a need to monitor their children constantly, wanting to know where the children are and what they are experiencing. So they spend a great deal of energy keeping up with their children. They watch them and interact with them, not only for their own pleasure, but out of their need to know what is affecting them.

The outside world worries parents because they see much of it as malign, and because they also see, probably correctly, that it is beyond their control. One example of this is powerful parental anxiety about the drug culture. Children's adolescence, a distant time for most of these young families, is etched into their minds as a future danger point, when powerful forces might easily undo the most careful child-rearing efforts. The sense of helplessness in the face of such forces is explicit in comments like Mrs Farlane's: 'In this society today, I think the greatest fear a parent has is that the child will turn to dope or something – I'm just afraid the wrong kids will get hold of them. . . . It's a terrible thing, but I feel this way – my only hope is fear. It's like teaching younger kids to be afraid of the street so they'll stay out of it – that's the kind of danger you're talking about. . . . I try to tell the kids – "Those kids who touch drugs, they're dead. Their life is over".' Even those ideologically committed to changing the structure of the family and child rearing feel these anxieties. Discussing her son's future, Mrs Parks, an advocate of change, says: 'I sort of see that if he goes on the way he's going now, he's going to be a really neat person. Only a sinister outside force would change him. . . . I'm so aware of the world changing so fast – who knows what he'll have to face in twenty years. He's going to see a lot. . . . He's going to have a lot to think about.' These concerns can result in a family's feelings of isolation: rather than being part of an organic social system, the families see themselves as struggling in opposition to the disorganizing forces abroad in the wider society.

In summary, the parents we interviewed found deep satisfactions and much to enjoy in rearing their children. However, they also face uncertainty about the appropriateness of their child-rearing practices from two sources. First, they share with other American families a cultural rejection of the past that springs from the society's belief in 'progress'. Child rearing in any post-traditional society presents uncertainties, and Americans throughout much of their history have felt they were raising their children to be different from themselves, preparing them for a future no one can yet see. Second, these dual-worker families are breaking with our customary family sex-role division of labor, which is strongly reinforced by the culture.[1, 2] Mrs Sedman, for example, wants to work, but remembers that when her mother worked during her childhood she didn't like coming home to an empty house. Mrs Farlane remembers her father's disapproval of her aunt, who worked. So, in addition to the uncertainties they share with other young families, dual-worker families worry about the consequences of what they are doing. In our society there are general and often contradictory feelings about what 'perfect' parenting should include – 'permissiveness' vs. 'spare the rod and spoil the child'. However, there are few guidelines for specific situations, and there are few generally accepted and available supports for young parents. This means parents are operating in a world with few clear guidelines, but with very high expectations for the outcome. Parents must fulfil their difficult roles with little institutional help, and must do so in the face of disorganizing and outright pathological forces in the world outside the home. Finally, as parents in dual-worker families, they must cope with increased demands on their own time and energy and with fears that they may be doing their children harm by breaking with tradition.

Roles: implications for fathers and mothers

The previous section looked at some of the general child-rearing issues facing both parents equally – acceptable child-care choices, evaluation of themselves *vis-à-vis* societal expectations, and concerns for the future. We turn now to the question of the division of parental and household respons- ibilities within the family, and to some issues that affect fathers and mothers differently. The problems are only partly logistical – who can be home at 3.00 p.m. to meet children returning from school, where to live to minimize travel time to work and how to arrange for child care in an emergency. Parents talked to us quite freely about problems of this sort. But underlying these practical questions were other issues, expressed with varying degrees of consciousness and comfort – what is the proper role of a father of young children, is it wrong for a young mother to want to spend some time away from home and children, what do others think about one's household arrangements?

Division of household and child-care responsibilities

It is clear that many of the husbands express a certain ambivalence about their wives working – not only because of a fear that this reflects badly on their ability to support their families but also because a working wife is more likely to press for help with child care and housework and is less likely to have surplus energy to attend to her husband's needs. And if she works she has the valid argument that as she contributes to being a 'breadwinner' he should reciprocate and contribute to the housework. The families reflect a range of responses to this pressure, from Mr Farlane. who feels that as long as his wife can do most of the household and child- care tasks she can work too, to Mr Park and Mr Tilman, who are self- consciously trying to work out equal sharing relationships with their wives, such that each parent carries about the same load of family tasks. The following discussion presents a description of the range of actual arrangements and an analysis of the feelings behind them.

In each of these families where both parents are employed there has been some effort to reallocate both household and child-rearing chores between mother and father. In general, given the abundance of counter- pressures to equal task-sharing – whether they be social or internal – which naturally accompany any attempt to break with a long-established tradition of the division of responsibility widely shared in the society, the wife is pretty much left having to take what help she can get, i.e. whatever degree of task sharing she and her husband are able to work out between them. In about a third of the sample families, the fathers provide some child care when the mother is at work. Typically, they take care of the children about three nights a week, starting in late afternoon, and serving supper. However, they assume little actual responsibility – the wives have planned and prepared the supper before leaving and will clean up the kitchen and any other mess when they return. Another group of fathers take a more active and responsible role when providing child care. In essence, they take over the role of the absent mother, doing whatever chores she would have done had she been at home then, including laundry, cooking and clean-up. They do this for periods ranging up to a three-day weekend. Some of these fathers provide the same services at times when the wife is home, recognizing that she needs a break. Finally, two of the couples are trying to be more egalitarian in their division of home and child-care responsibilities. They are consciously ideological about it and plan the division of chores carefully. The Parks, for example, alternate times for child care and cooking dinner. This degree of equality is possible, however, because each works only one-half time at his or her paid employment. In many other families the problem of task allocation is exacerbated because both adults work at demanding jobs, with the result that there simply is very little time in which to accomplish everything necessary; other families fall between these groups.

Perception of roles

Traditional roles as wives and mothers, husbands and fathers, seem extremely tenacious. Time-use studies indicate that the distribution of household work in dual-worker families is very little different from that in homes where the women do not work. For families like most of ours, with two or three children, the youngest a pre-schooler, husbands do very little more than husbands whose wives are not employed, wives do a half-hour to two hours less per day, and children's contributions are very small and do not change much with the employment of the mothers (Walker and Granger, 1973).[3] It seems likely, however, that many of the fathers in our sample do more at home than the average man in the time-use studies. Why do families with employed mothers stick so closely to the traditional household division of labor?

As we indicated in our discussion of child-care arrangements, the women of our sample expect a great deal of themselves as mothers. They keep their children's welfare at the top of their overall priorities, and in the forefront of their minute-to-minute concerns. For example, Mrs Henry feels it is important to be patient, gentle and not to raise her voice. She is upset with herself when she cannot maintain these standards of mothering and does not readily see that there may be circumstances which justify or at least explain their violation. In one instance, when their four-year-old daughter awoke early one morning, she cracked several eggs into a box of detergent, whipped the mixture into a paste, and plastered the front walls with it. Mrs Henry feels she should not have become upset and angry as she did. Other mothers had similar examples of what they viewed as 'irritability' on their parts.

Women's demands on themselves as mothers are combined with powerful demands on themselves as homemakers. Women's concern with cleanliness suggests there is a close relationship between cleanliness and being a good wife and mother, but it also means there are likely to be problems about task sharing with their husbands. Some wives seem to feel their husbands just can't do the tasks as well and they seem to end up as 'super-mothers' – trying to work and assume responsibility for all household and child-care chores. Cleanliness then takes precedence over the attempt to redistribute tasks. This in turn suggests that it may sometimes be hard for women to relinquish responsibility for their traditional home and child-care chores, while at the same time they need and want help in handling all the demands on them.

In most of our families – even those who tried most conscientiously to divide household chores – the task of housekeeping and looking after the child's welfare was ultimately the mother's responsibility. The husband might 'help out' extensively, might take over a number of traditionally 'woman's tasks' in the household, but the responsibility to make sure a necessary task got completed – either by herself, her husband or someone else – resided with the mother. Though most of the wives we interviewed spoke positively about the degree to which their husbands lent a hand around the house and with child care, we learned that the very use of the phrase 'helping out' told us a lot about the divisions of labor in the household, divisions perhaps so basic that they were not even discussed. The husband's role was not to do the dishes or clean the house – when he performed these tasks he merely aided in a task that was ultimately part of his wife's basic role. Just how very basic this wife's responsibility is is exemplified in a remark made by Mrs Henry, who had earlier gone on at great length to describe how good her husband was in taking charge of the children. When asked which of them takes charge when the children are doing something they're not supposed to do, Mrs Henry replied: 'I usually give the chore [dealing with the children] to my husband.' The chore is clearly, unspokenly hers to give and her husband does the chore only because she asks him to. She substantiates this in a further remark after she was asked what would happen if she didn't ask her husband to take over: 'Most times I think he'd wait till I took care of the situation.' It is not always clear to what extent this kind of situation is due to the father's lack of initiative in sharing home responsibilities or to the mother's unwillingness to renounce her position as chief arbiter of their children's behavior.

Fathers, on the other hand, expect to be breadwinners for the family, and are seen that way by others. Their job is to maintain the financial security of the family. And this is an increasingly difficult role in today's economy. A lay-off can seem a failure for a father. The inability to earn ever-increasing amounts also may be construed as a failure. While we have no detailed control data from a market sample of young couples, there was a marked tendency among the fathers studied to switch from job to job, until they had children. Since the infancy of their first child, they have remained in one job, regardless of low pay or dissatisfaction. Yet, in parallel fashion, the men's ambivalence about their wives' employment indicates that it is as difficult for them to relinquish sole responsibility for their traditional breadwinning chores as it is for the women to let others help with child care or to relax housekeeping standards. Interestingly, children perceive quite clearly the same role assignments, and concur that both the mother who works outside the house and the father who participates in domestic activities are 'helping out' the other parent in his or her role (Hartley, 1960, p. 91).

Most fathers participate in child care and child rearing more than housework and it is interesting to speculate why. First, there is probably more enjoyment in doing things with or for a child, in interacting with another human being, rather than with a mop and a floor. Second, society in general, and more specifically one's friends and relatives, put a premium on being a good parent, a good father, but one seldom hears of a good 'househusband'. There seems to be more consensus about the value of being a good father than there is about the value of husbands' help in housework.

The effect of these role definitions is reflected in the importance mothers and fathers attach to their failures to meet role expectations. Mothers express guilt and consternation when they lose their temper with their children, or when their housekeeping does not meet acceptable standards. Fathers excuse such lapses in themselves more easily, explaining that it is natural when a man comes home tired from work. On the other hand, most of the women we talked to accept lay-offs from their jobs with equanimity, while both mother and father rank a job loss by the father as a tragedy. This is, of course, not unrelated to the relatively higher pay received by men.

In addition to these private, inner doubts and anxieties, the fathers who are taking a more active role at home and the mothers who are looking for earning power and new interests outside the home have to contend with external pressures from the expectations of others. Mr Wyatt describes social counter-pressures to a more equal division of labor in the household. Mr Wyatt and his fellow workers talk about these things at work and he reports most do little to help their wives. When Mrs Wyatt describes what her husband does around the house at get-togethers of his fellow

workers and their wives, he reports: 'The guys want to kill me. They say
"You . . . . you're getting us in trouble!" Their wives say, "Does he
really?" and the men get really mad.' Mr Wyatt is caught in a difficult
situation – he is in trouble if he helps out because his fellow workers feel
it jeopardizes their position, but he is also in trouble if he doesn't, both
because he wants to help somewhat and because his wife wants him to
help even more. Mrs Henry's mother thinks her daughter should not have
to work. Mr Henry feels this, and says, 'Her relatives give me the down
look about her working.' Mrs Rose's male co-workers in one work situation indicated, in their responses to her inquiries about finding babysitters,
that if she needed a babysitter she should not be working.

These couples, then, are not simply fighting societal expectations. They
must contend as well with their own well-internalized self-conceptions as
husband–provider–father and wife–mother. Because very few of them are
armed with the reassurance of a self-conscious ideology, deviation from
those roles, even if only in degree, brings criticism and pressure from
those close to the couple, puts them in the position of being at odds with
their culture's prescriptions, and activates ambivalent feelings within
themselves.

Conclusion

In terms of practical and concrete aspects of child rearing, our dual-
worker families experience some difficulties and some advantages. For the
families we studied, the issues of child rearing when both parents work are
highlighted by their having relatively lower incomes than in dual-profession
families where the issues of who should and will do household tasks,
however undesirable, is sometimes dealt with by buying outside services.
Because they rarely can afford out-of-home child care, nursery schools,
household help, laundry done professionally, or ready-prepared food, the
need to make some personal accommodation to negatively valued work
is immediate and strong. This pressure towards self-reliance combines
with and is reinforced by strong cultural values on that trait, and the
members of families exhibited considerable inner strength. Communication
between spouses is frequent, and, in spite of their busy timetables, it is
evident that they have talked with each other a good deal about each
child and have discussed and negotiated in detail child-rearing issues that
have often in conventional families been left to the mother alone. The
added pressure of the mother's employment seems to increase self-aware-
ness. Because they are doing something perceived as out of the ordinary,
parents give it special attention. As a result of their willingness to communicate and their active concern for their children, these parents are

able to work resourcefully and constructively to raise their children as well as possible.

In their feelings about parental, spousal and work roles and responsibilities, the going is rougher. This is related to the backgrounds of our families. The women, for the most part, have not gone beyond high school, and had not planned to work after marriage and children. They have grown up thinking the primary, indeed the only, occupation of a woman should be her family. The men grew up sharing those expectations. Moreover, in many cases the men and women in our sample grew up in families in which their mothers worked out of economic necessity. It is often clear that as children the parents in our families had not liked their mothers' working. For them upward mobility means a wife/mother who *doesn't* need to work. It is a blow to the men's aspirations and a reversal of the women's expectations when the wife in fact chooses or feels the need to work. The net effect, over both generations, is that of preserving an essential stability in the conception of the wife/mother role, centered on child and home care.

It can be argued that our culture (and perhaps others as well) has far more elaborated criteria for mothering than for fathering: there is less agreement on what constitutes good fathering. Fathers, at a minimum, are expected to provide for their families and to serve as disciplinarians to their children. A man who does more than that – who spends time with his children, who helps with housework, who teaches his children – is somehow doing more than is expected, and is acknowledged to be an especially good father. Several of the men in our group described their own fathers as fitting the minimal model – provider and occasional harsh disciplinarian. They have reacted by deciding to take a more active role with their own children, and see themselves as more affectionate and involved than their own fathers were. In this situation fathers in our sample have moved away from the models provided by their fathers.

We have tried to point out some of the general issues for dual-worker parents and how these affect each other – traditional sex-roles, work orientation, parental investment, self-perceptions, reactions to families of origin, resources for help and advice in parenting, and cultural expectations about child rearing. This article has examined the importance of these issues in families under a particular set of pressures. We have been impressed with both the importance of these issues to family life and with the quality of the effort and self-examination of these parents in dealing with each issue.

Notes

The research reported here was funded by: National Institute of Education No. 3-3094, National Institute of Mental Health No. 24742, and The Russell Sage Foundation.

Laura Lein is principal investigator, Jan Lennon is administrator, and Maureen Durham, Gail Howrigan, Laura Lein, Michael Pratt, Michael Schudson, Ronald Thomas and Heather Weiss are research collaborators.

1 The extensive role of American mothers in child care, relative to women in other societies, is well-documented by cross-cultural research. For example, the comparative data from a recent anthropological study of six different cultures, *Mothers of Six Cultures* (Minturn and Lambert, 1963), show that the New England mothers of 'Orchard Town' rank far above all other societies on the 'proportion of time mother cares for infant and young child.'

2 Mead (1970). Mead's discussion of generational relations is helpful here, for she both notes the paradox of the co-existence in our culture of 'a deep commitment to development and change [with] a continuing resort to absolutism, which takes many turns,' and points out the psychological necessity of both traits (p. 65).

3 Table of hours/day spent on housework

	Unemployed mother			Employed mother		
	Husband	Wife	Children	Husband	Wife	Children
Two young children	1·6	8·2	0·3	1·7	6·2	0·3
Three young children	1·4	8·0	0·6	2·1	7·5	0·4

Source: Walker and Granger (1973).

Bibliography

Hartley, R. E. (1960), 'Children's concepts of male and female roles,' *Merrill-Palmer Quarterly*, 6, pp. 83–92.

Holmstrom, L. L. (1972), *The Two-Career Family*, Cambridge, Mass.: Schenkman.

Mead, M. (1970), *Culture and Commitment: A Study of the Generation Gap*, New York: Doubleday.

Minturn, L., and Lambert, W. (1963), *Mothers of Six Cultures*, New York: Wiley.

Rapoport, R., and Rapoport, R. N. (1971), *Dual-Career Families*, Harmondsworth: Penguin.

Walker, K., and Granger, O. (1973), 'Time and its dollar value in household work,' *Family Economics Review*, Fall, pp. 8–13.

Whiting, B. (1972), 'Work and the family: cross-cultural perspectives,' Prepared for Women: Resource for a Changing World, an invitational conference, Radcliffe Institute, Cambridge, Mass.

6

Choosing Child Care: Many Options

Mary Rowe

'We're going to get married while we both finish up in engineering,' said Roger, bringing in Anne, his fiancée. 'We want to marry, and probably to have one or two children and we want to know how to combine careers and parenthood. Also we want to know what is best for the children . . . how should we take care of them?' Most people Roger and Anne's age are asking these questions. They are finding many different answers. Answers for parents can be many and various, for they depend on people's values, on people's jobs, on resources and friends and relatives available. And 'what is best for the children?' is also not easy to answer. Above the level of flagrant abuse there appear to be many acceptable answers as to what is best for children.

How to combine various jobs with having children used to be a pretty straightforward issue for most couples. The tendency was to follow one fairly standard pattern; a few people varied it a little; fewer varied it a lot. This meant that in most husband-wife families – perhaps 80 per cent of them – there were two or three or four or more children, with the father as the only breadwinner, except for pin money brought in by the mother for work done at home. Other less frequent variations included the mother in part-time or full-time work outside the home.

In the 1980s in the USA, all indications are that there will be many different, basic child-care patterns built around changes now manifest in labor force patterns and fertility. This article discusses some of the changes in society which mean new child-care patterns are developing. Then there is a description of the many different child-care arrangements in existence today (though these are still far from uniformly available as options). This is followed by a brief discussion of the pros and cons of various arrangements and how to choose among them.

To begin with, the full-time labor force participation rate for men has been declining. It may be down to about 70 per cent by 1990, for a basic 30–35 hour week. This means that only 70 per cent of all men aged 16–65 will be in paid, full-time work or looking for work, at any given time.

Others will be in training, on leave, early-retired, out-of-work, or working as fathers and househusbands.

On the other side of the coin, the labor force participation rate for women has been increasing. It will probably be at least 70 per cent by the 1980s counting part-time and full-time employment. Thus paid work patterns for most women will be increasingly similar to those of most men for most of their lives. This will be especially true for the probable one-tenth of all women who will never marry and the 10 to 20 per cent who we expect will have no biological children. We expect that perhaps another 50 per cent of all women will have only one or two children; they too are likely to lead working lives much more like those of their men than has been true in the past. These groups taken together will establish a mode of paid work for *all* women very different than the traditional mode of the 1950s.

Already the modal family has changed enormously. In place of the traditional male-as-sole-breadwinner family (which now accounts for only a third of two-parent families in the USA), nearly half of all husband-wife families now have both spouses in the paid labor force. In addition to these extraordinary changes in labor force participation we will probably see a further great change in family economics. From the 30 per cent of family incomes brought in by US wives in 1975, we will probably see 40 per cent brought in by the women of the 1980s. And probably at least a fifth of all wives will earn as much or more than their husbands.

Changes in marriage patterns toward divorce and unusual family forms are expected to continue into the 1980s, although families as such seem here to stay (Bane, 1977). I estimate that in the 1980s at least half of all children will spend at least two years of their childhood in a 'non-traditional family'. Most of these will be living during such periods with single parents. At any *given* time, probably 75–80 per cent of all children aged 0–16 will be living with two parents, or with parents and step-parents. However, probably more than half will have lived in a family different from the traditional nuclear type for a significant period of their early lives.

All these changes may be expected to occur in the context of very swiftly changing values about men and women. We expect that in the 1980s it will be widely accepted that women are equally, or nearly equally, financially responsible for their families. These changes will be fostered and acknowledged by equal rights laws. Both men and women will become step-parents in very large numbers. Possibly as many as half of all children will know a temporary or permanent step-parent at some point during their childhoods; possibly a third of all parenting adults will live with a step-child at some point. We cannot know exactly what the prevailing practices will be about the financial responsibility of mothers, but it seems likely that divorce and remarriage of custodial mothers will result in a further acceptance of the idea of equal financial responsibility of *all* women, including those in two-parent as well as one-parent families.

By the same token, our values about men and home-making and child care seem to be changing rapidly in some segments of the population.[1] The earlier stereotypical view was that marriages might, for a variety of reasons, have both parents in paid jobs, but it was presumed that such marriages would not, on the average, be as happy as where mothers stayed home. Moreover, early research findings indicated that most couples assumed that in most circumstances mothers would remain chiefly responsible for home-making and child care even if they also held a paid job. There have, of course, always been many exceptions, but a large number of American men now appear to have been changing their views very rapidly in the 1970s. A 1976 Gallup poll reports that men who believe in relatively egalitarian marriage are now far more likely to report their marriages as 'very happy'. And a fair amount of evidence, including this same poll, indicates a considerable shift for about half of American men toward egalitarianism.

In the 1980s more men will become single-parent fathers through death, divorce and adoption. (The proportion of single-parent males has already increased to about a tenth of all single parents.) Family patterns will also change due to the sharp increase in the number of wives who are major or chief breadwinners. All these facts will mean that the social and legal rights and expectations of men with regard to child care may be expected to continue to expand during the 1980s. Thus changes in labor force participation, in fertility, marriage, divorce and sex-role attitudes have combined to permit very wide ranges of child-care patterns and customs.

Child-care arrangements in the early 1970s

Recent nation-wide surveys of child-care arrangements illuminate the very wide variety of child-care patterns now existing. By and large, they vary by age of child, by type of parental employment, by family income, number of children and arrangements available.

To begin with an examination of the traditional norm (that mothers are the chief or only child carers), we find that most mothers *are* basically responsible for the children, although few are completely alone in this endeavor. Only about 3 per cent of all households have a child under 10 and use *no* form of care besides the mother in her own home (Unco, 1976).[2] And only 7 per cent have a child or children aged 10–13 and report no child care at all. In other words, nearly nine-tenths of all households with children under 14 do use some kind of care, once in a while, other than the mother in her own home.

However, many use very little care other than the mother. About a third of all parents report using care very briefly, for only about an hour per week. Another 30 per cent use care 1–9 hours per week. These brief arrangements usually involve the spouse (52 per cent), an older sibling (30 per cent), relatives in their own or the child's home (33 per cent, 27 per cent). Others include babysitters (26 per cent) and the child alone at home (12 per cent).

Thus, in about 75 per cent of all homes with 0–13-year-olds the mother is the principal and essentially the only caretaker. This is clearly the dominant mode of American child care. This dominant form is mitigated in a major way only by hours children are in school, from age 5 or 6, and by the brief babysitting hours, described above, totalling fewer than 10 hours per week. Of the remaining quarter of all families with young children, 10 per cent of the children are in care 10–19 hours per week, 4 per cent for 20–9 hours per week, 2 per cent for 30–9 hours, 6 per cent for 40–9 hours and 3 per cent for more than 50 hours. This group constitutes the second major mode of child rearing.

There are two major recent sources of data on the kinds of child care used in two-career families for pre-adolescent children in the USA. The Unco study examined all households using at least 10 hours of care per week and concluded that only a third of the mothers in these households were in paid jobs. (Others may have been in school or training.) The major types of care used by the households in this study were a relative in the child's home or another home (20 per cent and 25 per cent) and care by a non-relative in the child's home or another home (16 per cent and 20 per cent), for a total of 81 per cent of all care more than 10 hours per week. Another major study also looked at care over 10 hours per week for 0–12-year-olds, whose mothers were all in paid work. Here again relatives (including siblings) accounted for 32 per cent of all caretakers, non-relatives in the child's home or another home for 37 per cent of all care, for a total of 70 per cent (Duncan and Hill, 1975). The Unco study, and comparison of the two studies, indicate that relatives are somewhat more likely to be child carers for children whose mothers are not in paid employment. But in any case, family is plainly still very important in American child-care arrangements. And families and neighbors combined account for a very high proportion of all child-care hours.

Reading both of these studies and other available data (see for instance Levine, 1976) suggests that in about 10–20 per cent of all households where both parents are employed, that parents *share* much of the child care. Two-parent homes with a primary househusband are quite rare – under 5 per cent – but homes where men account for substantial child care are now a distinct mode.

Day care appears to be somewhat less prevalent than many observers might hope or fear. Recent studies find all *formal* child-care arrangements, taken together, to comprise not more than 8 to 10 per cent of all arrangements, and not more than 20 per cent of all major arrangements (those over 10 hours per week). Day care (including nursery school, Headstart, before and after school programs, as well as programs called day care) is a *major* source of child care only for pre-school children with mothers in paid employment in the rather rare areas where such care is available.

How to choose a child-care arrangement

How should a young couple choose? One is tempted to answer: 'Without too much concern.' Of course parents should choose child arrangements with thoughtful care, finding as many possibilities as they can, and then learning all the details about each possibility. But no one should feel bound to seek the 'one right method,' or to feel that any given, careful decision needs to be permanent.

To begin with, most people change arrangements several times. Most parents arrange in-family care, or care by relatives, for infants. For children between one and two, many parents begin to use a different kind of care, often because the major caretaker has gone back into paid employment and needs more hours of care. As the child becomes a pre-schooler, parents may switch again, often seeking some hours in a formal arrangement, especially if the mother is in paid work. This happens in part because the parents seek a social life and educational setting for their child, especially if it is a first or only child. Counting all kinds of care in addition to the mother in her own home, at any one time 36 per cent of all parents use one kind of child care, 30 per cent two kinds and 34 per cent three or more different kinds of arrangements (Unco, 1976).

Cost and distance from home are major considerations. About two-thirds of all households pay no cash for child care, but many arrangements are reimbursed in kind; only about a tenth of all arrangements are considered 'free.' And probably half of all substantial arrangements (more than 10 hours) are not cash-paid. Despite the fact that several studies find cost reported by parents to be a 'secondary' consideration, it is clear that actual behavior in choosing child care depends very much on the price of care. With respect to distance from home, about 80 per cent of all child care occurs within 10 minutes of home; fewer than 5 per cent of all parents travel as much as 30 minutes from home for a child-care arrangement. Thus most parents seem to include considerations of time, money and distance with great care.

Another important problem has to do with the reliability of child-care arrangements. Parents in paid employment place a high premium on arrangements which do not break down. The Michigan study indicates that in practice, arrangements made by employed parents break down only very rarely. In-family care and relatives appear to be the most reliable of care, with 'child takes care of self' and 'babysitters' found to be less reliable (Dickinson, 1975). This may be one reason why care at home with relatives is nearly universally reported to be the most satisfactory (Unco, 1976). However, it is important also to note that there is a clear and separate mode of parents who prefer child-care centers (and their variations) even though sick children often cannot go to them. This is presumably because of the educational and social advantages many parents find in these formal programs.

How important is the availability of different kinds of care? Studies differ on this subject. Some investigators believe that parents who want and need paid work will find some kind of child care, willy-nilly. These authorities, basing their argument on the assumption that observed behavior reflects preference, believe that the 'availability' of child-care options has no real effect on parental labor force participation. On the other hand, there is some evidence that most parents who prefer and can find a free arrangement, a relative, or who decide that they could themselves split child care, are already doing so, but many who would like to use more formal child-care facilities if they were available have not been able to find them (Dickinson, 1975). The Unco study also estimated that perhaps a fourth of all users would change arrangements if they easily could. These data indicate substantial potential demand for more care, for better care and for different options.

Effects on children and parents of child-care arrangements

There are no easy answers as to which child-care arrangement is 'best' for children. This is partly because it is very difficult to measure any kind of different effects related to specific responsible arrangements. Above the level of child abuse, it is almost impossible to find lasting differences among children who have experienced different arrangements. This is true for a variety of methodological (measurement) reasons and because most children are very adaptable (Rowe, 1976). Such evidence as exists suggests that children thrive best when their parents are satisfied with their work lives and child-care arrangements, and when the caretaker is stable and responsive (Howell, 1973). Obviously, it is enormously important that parents be truly well-informed about a variety of arrangements in order to choose wisely. It is also important that parents continually monitor child-care arrangements in order to prevent abuse and ensure responsiveness to the child's needs. Within any kind of care arrangement, including ideally selected ones, there can be abuse. Moreover, children and care facilities change, not to mention the parental pattern into which the care arrangement is being fitted.

Which child-care arrangement is best for parents depends on a wide variety of factors. We know that there are many parents who stagger their paid working hours completely in order to care for their children. These parents widely report themselves very dissatisfied with their arrangements, often feeling very lonely indeed, with little waking or sleeping time to share with their spouses. On the other hand, some 'split arrangement' parents, who use an additional child-care arrangement and see each other regularly, are among the happiest parents. Many parents who are essentially in the traditional mode, with the mother as sole caretaker, report themselves much happier about their children's welfare than they would be in any alternative arrangement. Many others would prefer more relief or more time in paid employment. Parents of children with special needs have a particularly serious need of outside support.

The Unco study reported that about half of all parents who would like to change their child-care arrangements would prefer a formal arrangement such as a day-care center. Many others who would like a change but not to day care, have children under two, and would prefer to change to in-home care, preferably with relatives.

Costs and benefits of choosing the egalitarian mode

The traditional mode and its variations are by now rather well understood. The husband's career comes first in the constellation of both spouses' use of time, and the husband will try to maximize his opportunities, promotions and salary in paid work. Both husband and wife concentrate on his schedule and needs; there need be no conflict between her career and his, although there may be some conflict between the two spouses over time spent with the family.

If Roger and Anne choose this model, Roger is likely to allocate his time in whatever way will best advance his career. His time in the home and with children will depend on his work, not on Anne's work or on how many children they have. If Anne, the wife, chooses paid work at all, it will probably be after she stays home for a year or more with the children. She will do nearly all the home-making. When she does take up paid work, she will, all in all, work 7–10 hours more per week than Roger, counting all paid and unpaid work and commuting. She will also get less sleep than he but will probably have a more leisurely life during some of her hours at home. How she will allocate her time will depend mainly on

Roger's day and the children. Her career will be considered secondary, at least until the last child is well on his or her independent way.

But if a couple like Roger and Anne opt for a more egalitarian mode, as a great many US students assert that they wish to do, they will have another kind of cost-benefit reckoning to do, in terms of risks and potential benefits lying ahead. If each of them can find half or three-quarter time paid work, while the children are small, the family will receive one or one-and-a-half salaries for these years. Suppose each parent works 30 hours a week in a paid job. Suppose further that they use child care 20 to 30 hours per week, including evening babysitting, and that otherwise they split homemaking and child-care responsibilities by dint of some job-staggering. They will each get to know the children and the skills of home-making; they will have a chance to spend some time alone together, and perhaps even some time at church activities or volunteer work.

These spouses will probably have a much keener sense of each other's lives. The typical 'learned helplessness' of each sex toward the other's role may never develop in Roger and Anne's marriage. As they share responsi-bilities they may feel much less taken for granted and less lonely than many fathers and mothers. Anne can still be very supportive of Roger's need to relax after the office though she works herself; and Roger can still help out in Anne's areas of domestic responsibility as well as some of his own.

Their family financial security, as well as actual income, will grow more rapidly than if either one were the sole family breadwinner, as lifetime earnings and the ability to find and keep a job depend much more on continuous years in the labor force than on hours per week. Promotions will probably come later for Roger and Anne than for full-time workers. However, each can expect much higher life-time earnings than if he or she drops out for very long for family responsibilities. Thus, despite their expected later promotions, egalitarianism permits much higher (and more secure) family earnings. Though the strains of keeping two jobs going, as well as domestic responsibilities, may restrict their external activities in some ways, we would expect that the quality of life for these two may nevertheless be good; each will have several arenas for friends, status, productivity and self-image. Both spouses will have work areas, at home and in volunteer work, where there is considerable autonomy over one's work. Anne may get more sleep and more recognition than if she lived a traditional life; Roger will gain more options for self-expression and perhaps a respite from the competition at work.

If either is left alone, through death or divorce, he or she is more likely to survive in both paid work and family life. (Men who equally care for their children have, in practice, more rights with respect to custody and visitation.) One can imagine that, when Roger and Anne retire from child raising and paid work, they will be much more comfortable under circumstances where they both have a wider range of skills and interests. Their mid-life crises may also be less severe, with a wider range of options offered by two sets of skills and two incomes in the family.

Many couples may choose to share family responsibilities this way so completely that neither spouse ever drops out of school or job for family reasons. But other couples may choose to have one or the other spouse a full-time home-maker for a period of time and to alternate who is staying home. And many couples may need to have both in full-time paid employment, using child care 30–45 hours per week, at least until the youngest child is in school. The important question is the decision, early on, to share home-making, financial responsibility and child care. Many couples seem to be making the new model work very well.

How to choose a child-care arrangement

Ideally a couple would begin discussing child care as they begin discussing life together. In the opinion of this author, decisions about child-care arrangements are the most fundamental decisions a couple will make in terms of the roles they will occupy in and out of marriage for the rest of their lives.[3] These decisions, especially if the couple has more than one child, are likely to predict how both partners will spend their time for at least 10–15 years.

A couple anticipating a birth will want to take stock of the parents' careers, of their present and anticipated incomes, of all the possible child-care alternatives and of their places of residence and work (in relation to commuting to work and to care arrangements, if any).

They should discuss all possible relatives and friends, and visit and discuss all available alternatives, including trading child-care hours with friends. Many couples may even consider moving or changing schools or jobs to permit easier care arrangements. The major elements of choice will be time of commuting, price of care, reliability of care and special elements of care that a given child may need at a specific time. The price of care should carefully be balanced against the life-time earning expectations of a spouse that would otherwise stay home.

Most communities have libraries and community health programs with access to Day Care and Child Development Council[4] materials on how to choose child care, how to monitor arrangements, how to evaluate or even become a family day caretaker, how to begin a play group or child-care center, on how to find lists of local child-care facilities, including those with particular ethnic or other characteristics. In the United Kingdom this kind of information is available in libraries, social services offices and community health centres. Reading and talking with local experts is most important in cases where parents and/or children have special needs.

All young parents should keep two major rules in mind: their children are much likeliest to thrive if the *parents* are happy about their work and child-care decisions, and if the care takers are stable, responsive and consistent. Bystanders can nearly always safely be ignored.

Summary

Young couples, such as the hypothetical one described, would do well to undertake a flexible, careful and continuous examination of child-care options. They should have available plans for several different arrangements at any given time and over time. Most probably they will consider a variant on the theme of Anne as chief care taker, but not necessarily. If their marriage is egalitarian, they will find more and more of the law, and more and more young couples, agreeing with their values, and their chances of a very happy marriage may be greater. If they decide for the use of child-care arrangements, the number of hours they use child care will probably depend on how the caretaking parent(s) spend their time. The type of arrangement will vary with age of child, price, distance from home and the number of children they have. The effects of their child care arrangements, if the arrangements are stable, responsible and carefully chosen, will depend more on the parents' values, attitudes and behaviour than on the specific care arrangements.

Notes

1 See for example, Fein (1976), Levine (1976), Pleck (forthcoming), Rowe (1976), and the new panel data from the Institute for Survey Research at Michigan.
2 Unless otherwise specified, detailed data in this article are from the Unco Study.
3 For a further statement of this point of view, see Dinnerstein (1976) and Rowe (1977).
4 The Day Care and Child Development Council of America, Inc., 1401 K Street N.W., Washington, D.C. 20005.

Bibliography

Bane, M. J. (1977), *Here To Stay: American Families in the Twentieth Century*, New York: Basic Books.
Dickinson, K. (1975), 'Child care,' in G. J. Duncan and J. W. Morgan (eds), *Five Thousand American Families*, vol. III, pp. 221–32, Ann Arbor: Institute for Survey Research, University of Michigan.

Dinnerstein, D. (1976), *The Mermaid and the Minotaur, Sexual Arrangements and Human Malaise*, New York: Harper & Row.

Duncan, G., and Hill, C. R. (1975), 'Modal choice in child-care arrangements,' in J. Duncan and J. W. Morgan (eds), *Five Thousand American Families*, vol. III, pp. 235–58, Ann Arbor: Institute for Survey Research, University of Michigan.

Fein, R. A. (1976), 'First weeks of fathering: the importance of choices and supports for new parents,' *Birth and the Family Journal*, summer, vol. 3, no. 2, pp. 53–8.

Howell, M. C. (1973), 'Employed mothers and their families—I,' *Pediatrics*, vol. 52, no. 2, August, pp. 252–63.

Howell, M. C. (1973), 'Effects of maternal employment on the child—II,' *Pediatrics*, vol. 52, no. 3, September, pp. 327–43.

Levine, J. A. (1976), *Who Will Care For the Children?—New Options for Fathers (and Mothers)*, New York: Lippincott.

Pleck, J. H. (forthcoming), 'Men's roles in the family: a new look,' in C. Safilios-Rothschild (ed.), *Family and Sex Roles*.

Rowe, Mary P. (1976), 'That parents may work and children may thrive,' in N. Talbot (ed.), *Raising Children in Modern America, Problems and Prospective Solutions*, Boston: Little, Brown, pp. 286–303.

Rowe, Mary P. (1977), 'Child care in the 1980's: tradition or androgyny,' in J. Chapman (ed.), *Women into Wives*, Beverly Hills: Sage Publications.

Unco (1976), *National Childcare Consumer Study: 1975, vols I–II: Basic Tabulations, Current Patterns of Child Care Use in the United States, American Consumer Attitudes and Opinions on Child Care*, T. W. Rodes (principal author). Prepared under Contract #HEW 105-74-1107 for the Office of Child Development, H.E.W., Washington, D.C.

7

Commuting

Agnes Farris

One problem frequently encountered by dual-career couples is the lack of geographical mobility of one partner because of the career commitments of the other. The lack of freedom to relocate constitutes an obstacle to upward mobility and often a source of frustration to the career-minded to the extent that it restricts the individual from pursuing every available opportunity to develop a career. The career opportunity may appear in the form of an unusually exciting challenge, new responsibilities with promising career prospects, a higher pay, higher status job, or simply a good professional education. Unlike the single or the married colleague with a non-working partner, the professional with a working partner cannot exploit these opportunities at will. He or she has to give careful consideration for the future of the other career in the marriage partnership in any such major career and home location move. In many circumstances, the new location does not offer the partner any career choice at all. This conflict between career and family, or between two careers, is often difficult to resolve.

The conventional solution to this problem of dual-career co-ordination is compromise – one or both spouses taking less desirable jobs or one spouse giving up working altogether. The latter is not uncommon, and in almost all cases the wife is the one who compromises. This is the case because in our present day society, while there is an acceptable role of an unemployed educated wife and mothers, the equivalent for the husband is practically non-existent. In these circumstances, the wife's career suffers.

One unconventional approach to resolve dual-career conflict is to adopt the commuting lifestyle, exemplified by husband and wife living and working separately in two different cities during the working week, and re-uniting over the weekend. This lifestyle has drawn considerable general interest, primarily because of its seemingly radical departure from the conventional married lifestyle. However, it deserves a more serious look than just another contemporary lifestyle because it may be a viable alternative to the conventional solution of compromising one or both careers to resolve the dual-career conflict. The lifestyle constitutes a solution to the dual-career co-ordination problem to the extent that it permits each spouse to pursue a career independently of the geographical restraints imposed by the career demands of the other, and at the same time, maintain an ongoing marital relationship. With rising numbers of women with professional qualifications and increased employment opportunities for women in a variety of professions, the search for similar solutions to the dual-career co-ordination problem seems the more critical.

Very little is known about various aspects of the commuting lifestyle except from occasional brief and sketchy case descriptions in the news media. Questions such as why these people commute, how they decided to commute and what are the pros and cons of commuting remain unclear. As an attempt to explore some of these issues, I did a study in 1974 interviewing ten commuting couples of varied professional and family backgrounds. The purpose of this article is to examine the choice of commuting in the various circumstances and to analyse some of the issues confronted and solutions evolved. The kinds of questions I will address are as follows: What sort of people are they? Why did they make this decision? What about child-raising – do the children suffer? What are the attitudes of friends, relatives and colleagues at work? What are the non-economic as well as economic and career benefits of this arrangement to them as people? What is the impact on the couple relationship and on family life? In other words, what are the major advantages and disadvantages of the commuting lifestyle?

First, briefly on the personal backgrounds. In the sample studied both husbands and wives had high educational qualifications. All except two had graduate training. Eight were university professors, one an instructor; four were vice-presidents in industry, university or foundations; three were professional consultants; two were lawyers and one a manager in business. In this sub-group where the men were holding high-income and high-status jobs, the wives were not discouraged from or uninterested in seeking careers of their own. On the contrary, their own outstanding qualifications and the attractive career opportunities available to them provided the stimuli for the decision to commute. Their jobs also allowed high work flexibility so that the marriage relationship could be sustained despite the strains of commuting.

A brief description of the commuting lifestyle at this point would help in understanding the following discussion of its pros and cons. The typical commuting pattern is characterized by compartmentalization of work and home lives. During the few work days away from home, the commuter is totally involved in work – long hours, busy schedules, and full concentration on work without interference from family demands. During the weekend, however, time and attention are devoted to family oriented activities – spending time with husband/wife and children, and helping out in household chores. In the series of couples studied I found that even among these fairly untraditional couples who shared a lot in household responsibilities, the wife's weekends were often spent in household work and organization rather than in recuperating from the previous week.

The above pattern of total work and home segregation was fairly typical of the couples who commute weekly, but less apparent when the commuting was on a monthly basis, which was the situation of one couple.

One apparent disadvantage of the arrangement is the necessity to attend to all work or home activities in relatively short stretches of time. The resulting hectic schedules plus the commuting itself become sources of physical strain. However, the total segregation of work and home provides the commuters with great flexibility in their schedules when they are not at home. A few commuters interviewed expressed that they greatly appreciated their opportunities to devote long hours to work with no competing family responsibilities – a benefit not enjoyed by their counterparts in the conventional dual-career family.

Why did these people decide to commute? All of the ten couples studied in this series indicated that their commuting decisions were solely motivated by their career concerns. Their situations at the time of the initial decisions fitted into two patterns. Some had been in their professions for some time; others had just completed their professional training. For different reasons both sub-groups were unwilling to permit geographical barriers to preclude opportunities which would allow them to develop and utilize their skills.

For the younger couples there was a determination, particularly on the part of the wives, that they should not get diverted at a crucial stage in their career development – when they were ready to exercise the skills for which they had trained so long, and when they could see that a failure to gain a work experience could abort subsequent career development. For the older couples there was a feeling that the fullest exercise of their potentials, once again primarily amongst the women, was not yet reached. A wish to seize an opportunity, perhaps a rare one, to press for the advantages in it while they were still able.

While personal motivation and aspiration, family factors and career stage all play a part in setting up predispositions to accept such a commuting situation, the crucial determinant in the decision seemed to be the individual's perception of the critical character for them of the job opportunities available.

The elements which make a particular job opportunity seem critically attractive include the following: the low supply of suitable jobs locally; the uncertainty of future appropriate job opportunities; the outstanding margin of monetary reward in the 'away' job; the prestige of the position or institution offering the job; the personal challenge felt to be present in the job as compared with local opportunities; the particular persons involved, and their attractiveness as colleagues; the future potentials in the 'away job' situation, for which the specific job may serve as a testing ground or toehold for a possible whole family move.

For most of the couples, the preferred alternative would have been for comparable career alternatives near home. Typically the local job opportunities are absent or clearly inferior to the ones made possible by commuting. One woman indicated that although she was dissatisfied with the commuting arrangement under which she saw her husband only infrequently, the alternative was no work, and therefore, possibly, an aborted start to her career. She had no regrets for having chosen a commuting alternative which provided her with a good start in her career. But in the absence of such options these people have accepted that for them it is more important for each to have a successful career than to see each other daily.

Probing into the decision-making process undergone in each case, I found it surprising that in all except one situation, the couples studied in this series took very little time and deliberation to choose commuting – a major change from their previous lifestyle – as their way to solve the dual-career co-ordination problem. One mother of two young children summarized her family's decision in these few words: 'We accepted the offer and then worked out the logistics.' This demonstrates the determination, the confidence in one's own judgment and capability and above all, the very strong career orientation shared by the ten couples. Perhaps these same qualities had contributed and would continually contribute to the career successes of these individuals.

Commuting creates a range of actual and potential problems – financial, emotional, logistical and personal. The nature and significance of the problems vary with family and career stages as well as with the particular situation of a commuting couple. The problems confronted by the couples in the series represent some of the key issues that commuting families in similar situations have to face.

Emotional costs present a set of issues. Commuters live separately from spouse (and children if there are any) when they are at work, and have little time to be spent with the family during the few off-work days. The regular and lengthy periods of separation from family members is probably the greatest deterrent for most dual-career families who may choose the commuting alternative.

The nature of the concerns and anxieties that the commuting couples had to confront and work through differed according to family stage. The younger, childless couples primarily expressed concern with emotional and interpersonal issues. Their anxiety tended to include fears about growing apart, about their partner getting sexually involved with someone else and the fear of divorce. Early in the experience there is often a feeling of loneliness, but characteristically the couples soon adjusted to the situation.

Sheer *degree* of separateness may be a factor in generating a negative reaction to the pattern. For example, one young couple who commute on a monthly basis expressed dissatisfaction with the commuting arrangement's affect on their marital relationship, while none of the couples who commute on a weekly basis expressed this. It is possible that dissatisfaction with the arrangement increases with the duration of separation. Different couples probably have different tolerances, or cut-off points, beyond which they experience significant dissatisfaction. This may vary with age, family stage and personality. I noticed that while some people indicated in the interviews that they are paying a very high emotional price for their careers, others did not seem to attach great importance in their self-conception to being *together*, as part of a close couple with daily interaction. Career opportunities seemed to be more important.

One potentially negative element is, of course, the risk to the intimate couple relationship itself. Younger couples in the group seemed to establish social relationships independent of their spouses, as opposed to older couples who preferred not to socialize independently. So, age is likely to be an influential factor, though far from a simple unilinear one. There may be issues of mid-life restlessness, and also complexities in couples' values in relation to how 'open' a relationship they wish to have and can tolerate. The younger couples' greater sociability may reflect their different values as well as their greater vigour.

While emotional issues were of the greatest concern for the young and childless couples, logistical issues centred upon housework and child care predominate among older couples with children.

One critical factor which enabled families with children to absorb the commuting pattern is the willingness of *both* members of the couple to abrogate traditional ideas of wife/mother's exclusive responsibilities for domestic and child-care work. I found in the series studies the spouses of commuting wives readily took a lot of child-care and household responsibilities.

Availability of good and reliable substitute child care is the major problem when children in a commuting family are young. While some form of day-care arrangement can be made, there is always the chance of something unexpected happening, such as a child or babysitter getting ill. In such circumstances the non-commuting spouse has to cope with work commitments and family demands at the same time. Good logistics and sometimes excess physical energy to deal with the situation become critical.

In the series studied, families with children at the time the commuting decision was taken were more likely to adopt the pattern as a permanent one in their family structure, despite the difficulties of arranging for child care. In contrast the couples without children in this series saw it as an interim arrangement within a definite period of time. Clearly the variations that will emerge require refinement of these observations.

One area of some concern is the effect of a parent's commuting on the upbringing of children in the family. When I raised the issue with commuting couples with young children, the overall responses were positive.

These couples sought indications that their children showed such desired characteristics as an increase in independence, resourcefulness, a feeling of competence and involvement in the widened range of interests exhibited by parents who both had active careers.

To the extent that I was able to make personal assessments of some of the children of the commuting families, my impression is that they were well adjusted to their parents' lifestyle and that the overall effect is at least arguably in the direction emphasized in the parents' evaluations. They all seemed to be healthy, independent, intelligent, capable and to have close relationships with their parents. The parents in turn seemed to be highly attentive and sensitive to the various needs of their children and to place great emphasis on the importance of being able to communicate with them. There was some evidence to indicate that they took special pains to foster these modes of parent-child interaction precisely because their career lifestyles put them at risk. Nevertheless, the presence of young children does tend to create difficulties in the commuting family due to lack of readily available child-care facilities in today's society.

The most commonly cited problem of the ten couples interviewed was the high financial costs of sustaining the pattern. Most of them earned sufficient income to cover costs of commuting in addition to other expenses, but not high enough to make the commuting costs insignificant.

The negative features of the pattern included the fact that financially the high commuting costs took away their capability of acquiring assets that might have been possible without these expenses. This was a factor of less concern to older, financially more established and better salaried couples than to the younger ones, who felt financially stretched in attempting to establish themselves. The fact that many of them commute with no major financial pay-off strongly suggests that the families commute less for monetary gain than for personal, career interests.

Few considered that the drain on physical energy incurred by frequent travelling was a major issue. Some commuters found their travelling tiring, but most indicated that the effect was minimal.

The couples interviewed absorbed various strains and costs and tended to report that there was little influence of commuting on their marriage. Though the tendency was to present an undamaged facade of managing well despite strains, it is too soon to be able to argue conclusively that the toll on marital relationships is negligible.

One factor in supporting the decision to establish a commuting working-couple pattern seems to be the ability of the couple to find and sustain supportive friends. With a few exceptions everyone in this commuting group felt that their friends were supportive of their efforts to pursue two careers and that this was important to them. They tend to avoid too much contact with people thought to be critical. While it is not fundamentally questioned when the male is the 'away' one, it tends to be more questioned when a female married professional, for example, commutes, particularly if she has children. Her spouse may encounter chauvinistic questions such as: 'How could you *let* her do it?'

Although the weekend is the only time when the commuting families reunite as family units, not all families limit their activities to family-centred activities. In fact, a few couples reported that their social activities were as much as before commuting was undertaken, while others reported a slight decrease.

One major drawback of commuting to a job, however, is the exclusion from the 'local scene' – the social network of the colleagues. The loyalty and commitment of the commuter to the institution are sometimes questioned. This could have an adverse effect on the individual's career future at the institution.

As discussed above, commuting incurs substantial financial and emotional costs, drains on physical energy, complicates household management and possibly poses threats to marital and family relationship. What benefits do commuting professionals derive from their sacrifice?

The largest single gain attained by the commuting arrangement is professional development. By undertaking this arrangement it is possible to exploit career opportunities that are rewarding and satisfying, and to maximize career prospects. Several commuters studied in this series reported deep satisfaction in having pursued the job opportunity which required their commuting. While some said that they were ready to look at alternatives, perhaps of lesser challenge, closer to home, others saw long-term prospects in their present jobs and were willing to absorb commuting as a permanent way of life. Overall, the evaluation of the worth of commuting was definitely positive.

Several people also mentioned the side benefit of total segregation of work from home – the opportunity to be totally free from family demands and concentrate on work while away from home. Some younger couples remarked on the chance for personal growth and development.

The commuter couples may be said to have strong career motivation, to be independent and self-reliant as individuals. The fact that they continued to do so for extended periods of time suggests that they are strongly motivated to develop their occupational careers. However, the importance of supportive attitudes and behaviour on the part of each spouse should be emphasized. The active co-operation of both is important to make the arrangement viable for any length of time; therefore, strong commitment to the marriage, basic trust in the spouse, openness and ability to communicate effectively, seem to be prerequisites for sustaining this type of marital relationship, with its frequent separations.

Other factors that are crucial for the operation of the commuting pattern include good health for all family members, a financial level which makes travel and associated expenses feasible, availability of good transportation and personal services, a high level of physical energy, and the capacity for an efficient organization of household and child-care activities. Added to these factors, satisfactory operation of the pattern seems to depend on a willingness to *try*, a determination to *overcome* difficulties, a large degree of *resourcefulness* and *flexibility* to adjust to new circumstances and an unwavering value commitment to both family and career.

The commuting lifestyle is a feasible way of living. The fact that at least some families with children have demonstrated that they were able to undertake it for two years or more without drastic damage to family functions is tangible evidence of the possibility. There was no reported gross negative influence on either the development of the children or of the marital relationship.

This study was only able to examine the career and family interaction of the ten commuting families at a certain point in time. A number of important questions remain unanswered: e.g. whether commuting significantly benefits career advancements of the individuals who commute; whether commuting has a slow erosion effect on all marriages; whether it benefits some; whether it is subject to different cut-off points of time and distance; what the effects are on the children, etc. Commuting for some may be a process in which very highly motivated and extremely competent people engage in the activities for a limited period of time. For others it may be a satisfactory stable balance in their structuring of work and family commitments.

The commuting lifestyle should not be seen as a viable alternative for *every* working couple. Almost all of the couples studied were cautious, though positive, when asked whether their lifestyle should be recommended to others. They qualified their answers with points concerning themselves, their spouses, the marital relationship, and practical factors. People who live apart from their spouses have to be independent and trusting; they must be resourceful and capable of tolerating separations (if not actually enjoying life more that way).

Therefore, this lifestyle should be seen as one of several ways to integrate career and family life. As more women actively pursue a career and as their expectations for professional success increase, the weekend marriage is likely to become a way of living for many more families. But it is still, and is likely to remain, a special case, suitable and feasible for some couples but by no means a general prescription.

8

Work Sharing: A Norwegian Example[1]

Erik Gronseth

The natural habitat of a society, of course, influences its social organisation. But, the precise ways in which it does so are mediated by the technological and economic structure of the society. The term *economy* refers, most generally, to the linkage between living organisms in societies and then the environments from which they, take resources to maintain and expand their life functions. Therefore, all plants, animals, water and air, other humans, and aspects of these which are organised for human use belong to the economic elements of the environment. *Technology* is the means by which work changes economic elements into usable resources. The wide variety of ways in which the human family and the roles of men and women are shaped is in decisive measures influenced by the ways in which economies and technologies are organised. So, we are concerned with this interplay. In western societies there is today growing discontent about the traditional and still pervasive family and sex-role patterns, as well as with their relation to occupational and economic life.

One approach to the issue of finding an appropriate structure of work-family interaction has been to relate different patterns of male or female authority and resource control to different types of economic situation. Generalisations beyond the obvious ones relating to male domination in warrior or other muscle-using societies are still being worked out. An early generalisation, by Engels, was that whenever production of economic goods gave a yearly surplus that could be accumulated as private property, the males took advantage of their superior power (relative to women) and developed a (more) patriarchal social system.

With the colonial, commercial and industrial expansion of the economic (and military) systems in western Europe and America, the feudal forms of the 6,000-year-old patriarchy of our civilisation changed into capitalistic forms with a generally new emphasis on differentiation between occupationally organised production for profit and socialisation of children and reproduction of the labour force within the family. Capitalism was founded, not only upon private ownership of means of production and upon 'free' markets for sale of the labour force and of the goods it produced by masses of dependent workers, but upon the drawing out of surplus value for the benefit of the private owners of industry. This economic structure had implications for the division of labour between the sexes, and for the structure of families as well as for the development of a social class mentality and of conflict of interests between the classes.

Under capitalism, the labour force became primarily male, partly as a consequence of factories legislation designed to protect women and children from the harsh conditions of early factory and mining work, and in order to secure an adequate reproduction of the labour force. Women were thus largely confined within the (then) nuclear family, partly to support and reproduce the males required in the labour force. Potentially women also had a secondary role as marginal and reserve labour. In capitalist societies – with some class variations – a woman's role is basically as a housewife in the nuclear family. The husband is employed, and therefore the provider. Housewifery involves reproduction, economic consumption, the provision of emotional support, as well as economic dependence and social subservience.

Wages are paid only for economically productive work outside the family while household services are not paid for. Housewives are only paid indirectly through their husband's wages and tax allowances. In exchange for her services her husband is legally obliged to support her and her children. The male, on the other hand, is not dependent on marriage for either economic support or for status, as regardless of whether he has a family to provide for or not, he is paid the same. Under capitalism, working-class women suffer a condition of 'double oppression', because of both sex and of class.

Of course, there are many variations as changes are occurring, in motivation, values and behaviour of men and women. Until the recent economic slump there was a demand for women to enter the labour market and to be educated comparably to men, and therefore to be able to command comparable positions in the economy. Consequently one now sees greater numbers of working wives and mothers with educational and occupational aspirations.

But the male–female wage differences remain, despite equal-pay legislation, and working women are concentrated disproportionately in part-time and short-term jobs, and among the low-paid employees. There is inadequate support, such as full-scale measures for day care of children outside the family. Family child care is still, for the most part, economically dependent upon the husband's – and increasingly also upon the wife's subsidiary – occupational work. Not even in the welfare state phase has capitalism seen fit to give regular pay for child care, especially not if done in the home. Few men are in part-time employment. Still fewer men take anything approximating half the burden of the productive work in the home, not even when the wife is also in full-time employment. What might appear as a shift from the husband-provider to a joint parental-provider role is usually merely a shift from the *exclusive* husband-provider role to the husband as the principal provider.

The husband remains an economic and status provider, tentative female dissents and protests notwithstanding. The socially and psychologically absent husband-father is the rule rather than the exception, as is the socially isolated and child-engulfed housewife, or alternatively, the double-role, over-worked, employed housewife with small children. These imbalances, anomalies, unhealthiness, oppressiveness and repressiveness, are, in my view, rooted historically in our patriarchal past and its present-day version[2].

But, as one looks to the future there is evidence of life-affirmative and liberating changes which break with this tradition. These changes are apparent in all points of the system – some people initiating, some following and some obstructing.

Some of these adaptations take the form of sex-role and occupational changes. There are also new family structures still within the framework of the traditional expectations but clearly pointing beyond them. These structures include communes and collectives, *and also the work-sharing family and occupational pattern.*

I use the term *work-sharing pattern* to refer to families in which the couple genuinely share work responsibilities, both within the home and in the occupational world. This may consist of different patterns. A couple may share the same job, or each may have a separate part-time job either in the same or different organisation. For the latter, the work-hours must be co-ordinated so that one spouse can be off work while the other is on. This arrangement may consist of sharing by the day, the week, or the month. The essential elements are part-time (rather than full-time) work, and equal sharing of domestic as well as occupational work.

In 1971 the Norwegian Family Council, a group of researchers, and several volunteer work-sharing couples, decided that a work-sharing family and occupational pattern was important to experiment with and study. It was seen as a strategically important, radical (albeit partial) change toward a more basically gratifying and balanced family and occupational life. This pattern was expected to contribute to a closer and more meaningful relation between the sexes, between the mothers and children, between fathers and children, between family and occupational life, between family and socio-political life – towards more constructively productive and less stressful occupational life – and towards lessening unnecessary consumption. It would be applicable to any couple, to those with no dependent children, those with children as well as to couples near retirement age.

Relative to the traditional family and to its burden on women, it would give the same advantages as would the dual-work pattern – it would salvage the mother from the mother-child isolation, and from monotonous household chores. It would give her a continuous occupational participation, on a basis equal to that of the work-sharing men. Discriminatory employment-practices against women workers would be less possible.

Furthermore, a work-sharing family pattern would do away with the husband-father's excessive occupational absorption and with his present peripheral position in family life. He would get relief from the stress and strain of being the main provider and of the competitive occupational life. He too would have the possibility for a broader and richer personality development and self-fulfilment, to develop his at present repressed and inhibited emotional capacities and potentials for human and emotional contact. The children would be salvaged from the personality stunting effects of the isolated nuclear family pattern. The boys as well as the girls would get intimate and realistic contact with an adult, loving male as well as female person.

While the children would get an equal amount of contact with both their father and their mother, the infants and toddlers would, under work sharing family conditions, avoid the experience of many contemporary full-time, dual-work patterns where the greater degree of parental separation results in spending seven or more hours a day in day-care institutions.

On the occupational side, this pattern would hypothetically mean more personally satisfied personnel – greater use of the potentials of women, and fuller use of machinery and workplaces.

On the theoretical level the work-sharing pattern is a special type of 'role sharing'. Role sharing is usually discussed with reference to a hypothetical idea of shared roles based on both spouses in full-time occupational employment, supposedly to be materialised in the so-called 'dual-worker' family. However, the empirical experience so far, in both western and eastern industrialised societies, is that role sharing is not reliably realised in this type of family structure when there is full-time work by both partners. The woman usually finds herself with the major part of the work burden and responsibilities at home. She remains in the primary housewife role along with her wage-discriminated occupational role.

As compared with the more traditional and moderately modern middle-class 'husband provider family', in which the wife is either a full-time housewife or has part-time employment, the dual-worker family implies a greater total work burden upon the spouses, and may actually increase stresses for all family members, the children included.

To improve the chances of the dual-worker family pattern resulting in genuine role sharing, one solution would be a total public and occupational takeover of all the main household and child-caring activities – more or less as in the Kibbutzim. But such an extensive capitalisation or socialisation of all the families as well as occupational services seems more out of reach in western societies than does the possibility for the part-time employment of both spouses.

The work-sharing pattern can, within the confines of capitalism, provide part-time jobs for women as well as men (given the absence of general mass unemployment). For each married male employee who would leave half his job, there could be available an equal half-time job opportunity for a married female (assuming, of course, the appropriate woman's qualifications). The work-sharing pattern thus appears generally to represent the only way within a capitalist economy to find secure, lasting and equal employment opportunities for both sexes.

Now there are, of course, other obstacles apart from capitalism and its need for a reserve labour force. There certainly are obstacles on the level of men's and women's expectations and societal attitudes and expectations, but these are subject to change. And there is the uneven income distribution, combined with the economic discrimination both against women and against families with dependent children. The latter circumstances make it less and less possible for average and low-income families to live on the basis of only one income, or on the basis of half a male plus half a female paid at 10–20 per cent lower wage level.

Thus, a general diffusion of the work-sharing pattern seems dependent not only upon part-time job possibilities for men and upon sex-role and mass psychological changes, but upon income equalisation, equal wages and massive public remuneration for child care.

The work sharing pattern should be regarded as a necessary, partial, but not sufficient condition toward a goal of universal roles and genuine equality between the sexes. In contemporary society it is a tiny minority pattern, but one that can be instructive.

Regardless of the possibilities for future large-scale adoption of the work-sharing pattern by public policy, by company practice and by individual families, it was of interest to encourage its adoption – and systematically to study the conditions under which it actually was adopted.

Norway's Family Council launched in 1971 a programme to propagate the pattern. At the Institute of Sociology, Oslo University, a research group was formed to look at the programme. The operational definition of work-sharing families was taken to be cohabitating heterosexual couples both of whom are gainfully employed on an average of not less than 16 hours a week and not more than 28 hours a week, combining their work hours in any way they saw fit. Couples to be included in the research project were limited to those with at least one child below school age (seven).

Altogether 16 work-sharing families, seven families who wanted to adopt the pattern but who found no employment possibilities, and five ordinary families, were, over a period of three-and-a-half years, located and recruited to the project.

By spring 1975, two of the families had been practising the pattern for about four years, six for half a year.

The experimental couples were obviously a select group of couples especially motivated for this work-family arrangement. For this kind of research and social purposes, this constitutes, however, no serious objection, since in future practice this kind of work arrangement will probably be relevant for a growing number of couples. It is interesting to find out how different kinds of families adjust to the new kind of work and family arrangement.

What obstacles, conflicts and frustrations were met with when adopting the work sharing pattern? What advantages and satisfactions were obtained – in the family, in occupational and social life? What internal and external family and sex-role restructurings were made? What were the effects of the new work and family pattern upon the family members' satisfaction and self-fulfilment – and upon their mutual emotional, power and work relations, as well as upon their and the family's relations to the surrounding society, all the way from kindred and neighbour relations to occupational and political life?

Here are sketched a few of the central propositions as to the expected 'effects' of the work sharing pattern. When being alone at home with the children half the ordinary occupational work hours we expected that the husband would come sufficiently close to the family's family events to become practically and emotionally involved and to actually take up something approximating half the tasks. He was expected especially to take on the ones that had to be solved right away, those that could not so easily be postponed until the wife came home. Otherwise it was expected that he would tend to take on the least traditionally 'feminine' ones,

Under these conditions the wife would be able to break loose of the spell of the housewife role, and even raise effective expectations to the husband of taking his share of the household chores and of the child minding.

This would result first in close to fifty-fifty sharing of the work burdens at home, and second, this would probably be done on an approximate role-sharing basis, so that the husband would take on a sizeable part of traditionally feminine family tasks, just as she had taken on half the traditionally male occupational and provider role by her half time in occupational employment.

A second set of hypotheses concerns the interpersonal family relations. As the wife would become economically more independent, she would feel the equal of her husband, not only economically and occupationally, but also in family matters. She would have more to give to both husband and children. Similarly the husband's new situation might be expected to give him more surplus energy for his wife as well as for his children.

The work-sharing pattern was expected also to reduce the relative isolation of the nuclear family unit. By way of integrating the husband-father in the internal family affairs and relieving him of occupational chores, he would probably be more motivated for extra-family activities on behalf of the family and its children. And a less isolated, moderately employed woman, stimulated by concerns common with those of her husband, was also expected to be motivated to take on external activities.

Most of the 23 work-sharing couples who volunteered for the programme were living in or near Oslo or in south-eastern Norway, but there were also a few in city and town regions on the west coast and in northern Norway. With respect to family composition and living standard all were ordinary small, nuclear families in their own or rented flats or houses, with mainly one or two children. In nearly all the families there was at least one child below school age and the parents were in their late 20s up into their late 30s. About half had a car and a deep freezer, nearly all had TV, vacuum cleaner and washing machine; all had modern sanitary equipment.

With the exception of a highly specialised older upholstery craftsman in public employment and his traditional housewife, all the couples were of the 'new middle class'. Close to one-half were lower-middle class, one-third were middle class, one-sixth were upper-middle class. Nearly all were white-collar workers and in public rather than in private employment.

Only four of the 23 wives were regular housewives prior to the choice of the work-sharing pattern. In close to two-thirds of the couples, the wife had a relatively lower occupational position – and lower education – than the husband.

As for the sex-role structure of the parental families, two-thirds of the women and close to one-half of the men had regular housewife mothers, the rest having had mothers with periodic or part-time employment.

A majority of the men came from families where either the father or the mother had been more or less 'absent' due to occupation, illness or early death.

Values and motives of work-sharing couples were of particular interest. The women were perhaps *more* than ordinarily oriented to having an occupational identity. Probably in part a consequence of their relatively high level of education the majority of the women had a very marked occupational interest. For most of them their housewife role appeared to come second to their occupational role, at the same time as they preferred not to have full-time employment while the children were small. Only one or two were *career* women.

The men respected their wife's desire to be occupationally employed, at the same time as they themselves were of either low or even negative in orientation to career commitment. The anti-career orientation was in a few cases combined with job problems, but all of the males in the study had a positive interest in their work.

Two-thirds of both the men and the women considered themselves to be somewhat or much radical in matters of equality between the sexes. Except for one man and one woman who considered themselves traditional, the other ones said they were of liberal orientation in these matters.

The reasons for choosing a work-sharing lifestyle varied. One-third of the men were motivated for their work-sharing choice by a problematic situation on the job which prompted them to reduce their occupational commitment.

Most of the wives as well as the husbands were of the opinion that parents should be the chief minders of their children; and this was a strong element in their motivation for their work-sharing choice. Nearly all the men chose the work-sharing pattern partly because of a strong desire to have close contact with their children, and to share child-minding joys and responsibilities with their wives. Some had such motivations because of special problems with the children.

For nearly all the women the wish for reduced time and responsibility with the children in order thus to obtain a better quality of relationship with them was central to the work-sharing choice, given that they did not want (or in some cases could not) leave the children in full-time day-care institutions.

All together the chief reasons for choosing the work-sharing pattern appeared to be: a concern for and interest in the children in combination with the wife's very positive, but moderate involvement in occupational work and the man's anti or moderate career-orientation, in some cases along with job-problems, and finally a desire for equality in their own relationship.

Only in very few of the families was there a strong active ideology of equality between the sexes, in such a way that their choice of the work-sharing pattern was part of their public campaign for this cause. For three-quarters of the men and for nearly all the women, some kind of explicit wish for equality between the sexes was, however, a part of the motivation.

In general it appeared that other practical and personal problems and motives were the driving forces for the work-sharing choice, sex-equality rationales coming essentially as a consequence of these other concerns.

Three types of sex-equality orientations were identified: (a) a *defence-orientation*, focusing on the circumscription and guaranteeing of rights and duties between the spouses; (2) *an autonomy and self-fulfilment-orientation*, focusing upon the possibility of each spouse for independent, personal self-actualisation; (3) *a communal orientation*, focusing on equality in and for the sake of togetherness, sharing, having things in common, doing and experiencing (especially the children) together. The three types were found about equally often among both sexes.

Couple-jointness and sharing was a conspicuous value for one-half of the men and one-third of the women; the wish to experience togetherness and harmony was part of their motivation. For one-half of both sexes the wish for a good or better marital relationship was the main motivation. One-fifth of both sexes mention specifically the hope for improved sexual relations.

The wish for personal fulfilment in areas other than occupation – in recreational or educational activities, or hobbies – was mentioned by one-half of the women, and by a large majority of the men. The men and the women took the first initiative for the work-sharing choice in about the same number of cases.

While for some of the couples the work-sharing choice was best under-stood as a positive effort to secure and continue harmony and sex-equality in the family, for others the work-sharing choice was more conspicuously related to the wish to get away from a negatively experienced situation; one that may even have reached crisis dimensions in relation to the children, to the job, to the woman's house- and child-work, or to the spouse. Altogether two-thirds of the families hoped to solve some such troublesome problems by means of the work-sharing pattern.

Only 16 of the original 23 families which wanted to enter the work-sharing situation did actually succeed in their intention. In one-half of these work-sharing couples the spouses work a full day approximately every second day, sometimes so that both are at work one day a week, the child being taken care of by someone else. In one-third of the couples one spouse works the first three days, the other the last two or three days, sometimes with the same one-day overlap variation as mentioned for the first type. Two couples share every day, but this makes for too much discontinuity. Two work every second week (the wives on a shift basis).

The majority work equal hours, usually from 20 to 22 hours a week.

Satisfaction with the pattern

Thirteen of the women and 12 of the men think the work-sharing pattern has fully met their expectations. The other ones simply had too great expectations about solving deep family or personal difficulties, or about getting time for large study or building-repair programmes (two of the marriages ended in legal separations during – but not because of – the work-sharing arrangement).

Three-quarters of both the men and the women mention problems con-nected with the work-sharing pattern, but two-thirds think they are minor ones. Economic problems are mentioned by only a few women and men. One woman and two men think they now have too much time at home together.

Some job problems are mentioned by eight women and seven men. A few complain they have had to take relatively uninteresting jobs or difficult work-hours in order to get a half-time position. Two of the women mention reduced career possibilities for the husband and themselves. Two women mention difficulties with keeping the contact with the others in the office. A few report some disagreement with the spouse about the work arrangement in their shared place of work. In two families they tend too much to bring problems of their shared work-place up for discussion at home. Only three report negative reactions from colleagues or relatives.

As for the task division at home, 13 women and nine men mention some problem in this connection, especially to begin with. One woman finds it difficult not to be too fussy and controlling about the husband's house-work. One husband thinks the wife is too meticulous, while another few say they have difficulties seeing all that needs to be done, and are surprised at how much time the housework takes.

Only one man has guilt-feelings for not using his time as meaningfully as possible, and only one other reported difficulty with his masculine identity or with taking on traditionally female activities.

In no family does the husband to any large extent use his time-off from the job for purely personal interests and pursuits. But more than two-thirds of both the men and the women report somewhat increased occasion for such interests.

In all 16 families the man takes at least a considerable part – if not always half – of the household and child-minding tasks. There appears to be just about equal sharing of the total home work-load in nine of the families. There appears to be a little overload for the women in four families, some such overload in two, and considerable such overload in one family.

As expected, equal-sharing occurred most often in the activities that were difficult to postpone, and in those activities that in society at large were not so clearly assigned to either women or to men.

Above all, the men tended to take an equal or even a greater share in child-minding activities, than in gardening, payment of bills, special and large purchases, preparation of meals and daily purchases.

Traditionally female tasks, such as house-cleaning, tidying, mending and washing of clothes, purchases for wife, children, and of lesser things for the house, were most often only to a limited extent taken over by the husband. On the other hand, the woman very seldom took any share in the traditionally defined male activities, such as repair of house, upkeep of the car, etc.

On a general question about sharing the responsibility for housework on the one hand and child minding on the other, 13 families reported equal sharing in the latter context, but only three in the former.

There is great satisfaction with the task division at home in ten of the families. In another two one spouse is 'very satisfied', the other simply 'satisfied'. In only two families is one spouse – the husband – less than satisfied.

The satisfaction with the responsibility sharing is not quite as wide-spread (six families are 'very satisfied', in two families the woman is only 'relatively satisfied' and in two she is 'unsatisfied'). Five women think the husband could very well have done more housework, house repairs and bill-paying.

Questions about who most often gets his or her way, in whose interest family life is mainly organised, who knows best about the family's economy, all point to a widespread equality in distribution of family power.

For five of the families both spouses say that there is now less domination of one over the other than prior to the work-sharing arrangement, ten say their family life is now organised more on equal terms, which means mainly in the interest of the children. Quite apart from the task and responsibility division, seven women and eight men say there is more equality between the spouses now than before, while most of the remaining families say they had equality also prior to the work-sharing arrangement.

Just about all the work sharers think their relationship to their spouse has in some important respect improved as a consequence of the work-sharing arrangement. A great majority find that they now have more time for each other. Improved solidarity or less conflicts are mentioned by 13 women and 11 men. More common interests and shared experiences and interests are mentioned by seven women and five men, 11 women and eight men mention increased mutual understanding of each other's situation and needs. Among these, three women and one man specify their more intimate relationship now than before, while four of each sex specify improved sexual relations. As mentioned, there has in some of the families also been an increase in smaller conflicts. In two families the work-sharing situation aggravated conflicts over work both at home and at the job. Two of these (one where the work-sharing pattern facilitated a largely friendly growing apart) came to legal separation.

Nearly everyone says there is now more time for and better contact with children – the father because he has more time and experience with them, the mother because she now has relief from them and does not get tired, being too overwhelmed by them. Two-thirds of the mothers specify that they now feel more joy with the children. Two-thirds of the fathers specify having better and more open contact with the children now and understanding them better. This does not exclude the possibility of the fathers more often being irritated over them than before, a fact mentioned by four. Nearly all of the couples consider that the children are the ones whose interests are best served by the work-sharing pattern. (There was no systematic information from the children themselves.)

The pattern of informal social relations with relatives, neighbours, friends and fellow workers appears not to have changed in connection with the work-sharing pattern. Only a few men report more contact with neighbours. The women who previously were housewives do, of course, report more fellow worker contacts, but this they could have obtained alone, without the husband being at home part time.

Only a few of the husbands do actually mention increased participation in neighbourhood and community organisation on behalf of children and the family. One husband has become a member of the local housewife association. (Only three of the women have such membership, while four others are active in local feminist groups.) Nearly all go to meetings in one or more professional, humanitarian or special interest association of which they are members, but not as a result of the new arrangement. Eight men and eight women do, however, say that they now are more active in associations or neighbourhood activities, and six couples say they have more occasion now to be politically oriented.

It should be noted that in a nationally representative survey in 1973 on attitudes concerning equality between the sexes, 38 per cent of the 450 married men and 45·5 per cent of the 450 married women said that if both spouses were to work equal hours in occupational life, they would prefer that both worked half time. This percentage was especially high among those with a family income below average and among the parents of small children. Twenty-six per cent of the married men and 20 per cent of the married women said it would be practicably possible for themselves and their spouses to go on half-time employment.

It seems safe to say that at least for families with small children with an average working man's income or higher, where both parents have above average education, where the wife has a firm and personal occupational commitment, where both are committed to the welfare of each other and of their children, and are strongly motivated for a work-sharing pattern, the adoption of this pattern generally results in the expected positive changes.

Mainly the families experience less strain and stress, better marital and parent-child relations than they did prior to adoption of the pattern, or as compared with what probably would have been their situation had they not adopted it. An unusual extent of equality between the sexes appears to have been achieved in terms of intra- and extra-family task division, power relations and role-sharing.

The 'two worlds of marriage' seem in decisive respects to have become one. The fathers appear successful in establishing contact with and caring for their small children, at least according to their own and their wives' standards.

Both husbands and wives appear more personally satisfied in their family and in their occupational life, in spite of minor new problems. With respect to work life, the important exceptions are the few who do get less interesting work due to present conceptions and organisations of part-time work.

Indications of increased neighbourhood and community participation can be found in some, but far from all, of the pioneering families.

The work-sharing pattern thus seems to be a viable alternative to the current dysfunctional sex-role, family and occupational patterns, although its large-scale adoption meets with serious structural constraints on the level of macro- and micro-economics, occupational, family and sex-role organisation and attitudes.

Whether strictly speaking the adaptations of the work-sharing families are effects of the work-sharing arrangement and/or of other previous or concomitant circumstances, is not easy to determine on the basis of this 'experiment'. To the extent the work-sharing spouses themselves report changes as due to the work-sharing arrangement, the likelihood is that this arrangement really is at least a central cause. But even where no specific change from before to after is reported, it is likely that for instance the reported equality in power and task division, the marital harmony and togetherness, etc., would not have continued had not the work-sharing pattern been adopted as a solution. In several cases, for instance, the work-sharing was adopted in response to the birth of a child, prior to which the parents had been able to maintain equality and harmony on a dual-work basis. The alternative to the work-sharing pattern would have been the husband in a full-time job, and the wife fully or partly at home, or perhaps fully employed, all of which – with the new child – would have resulted in a change towards a husband-dominated and wife-overburdened family structure.

The 'families' studied were on several important dimensions found not to be homogeneous. Apart from the work-sharing pattern they differed widely in terms of socio-economic and occupational background and attitudes to sex equality. The men differed widely with respect to career-orientation.

No blue-collar work family had adopted the work-sharing pattern. This is not because of a too low income, and not because part-time male jobs could not have been arranged, but probably because of the lower educational level and hence the lesser occupational interest and stability among wives of blue-collar workers, and because of their usually more traditional sex-role conceptions and values.

With an expected future increase in the educational level in families of blue-collar workers, motivation for the work-sharing pattern could also emerge among them. The cost of living may, however, continue to rise, so that more and more families, under continued demand for the female labour force, will become dependent upon one-and-a-half or two wages, so as not to leave open the work-sharing pattern as a family-economic possibility. In case of mass unemployment, however, the only way for married women to keep their jobs may be that men and women take half each of the remaining available jobs.

Improved economic conditions – especially for the low-income categories; substantial increases in children's allowances; sex-equal wages and general income equalisation, would, however, probably encourage the adoption of the work-sharing pattern.

Notes

1 This is a somewhat abbreviated and less technically styled edition of an article in *Acta Sociologica*, vol. 18, no. 3–4, 1975.
2 For a fuller analysis of today's family and of the dysfunctionality of the husband–provider role, see E. Gronseth (1973), 'The familial institution, alienated appendage to market society', in L. Reynolds and J. Henslin (eds), *American Society: A Critical Analysis*, New York: David McKay.

9

Job Sharing

William Arkin and Lynne R. Dobrofsky

Job sharing – 'dividing a job with each taking responsibility for half the total work – splitting the total workload of a single job' (Dickson, 1975, p. 244) – is developing as one new way of integrating and balancing the once separate domains of work and family. Job sharing for wages is particularly unique to the western experience, with its strong commitment to an ideology which emphasizes work and occupational status and wealth as primary goals. As a new work alternative, it takes several forms and is the result of employee initiation rather than employer or corporate experimentation in search of more productive and efficient work forms. Job sharing is permanent, high quality, part-time employment without the exploitive dynamics of low status, low wages, job insecurity and absence of fringe benefits which have been characteristics of most part-time jobs. Women, students, the unemployed, the handicapped and the elderly represent the principal subpopulations who have traditionally taken part-time employment. For the employee, the desirability of part-time employment has been the reduced time demand for work, the appeal of time and work flexibility.

In part, job sharing represents an attempt to institutionalize good aspects of the part-time work situation (flexible time) while eliminating the undesirable elements (economic exploitation). Additionally, job sharing is a response to a changed job market and to the strains confronting dual-worker families where the stress of managing the domestic situation often becomes critical when both must devote a major part of their energy to full-time employment.

The emergence of job sharing as an alternative work form required the combination of two social catalysts: one being the slow growth, post-industrial society and the accompanying economic crisis, particularly in the form of a tightening job market, and the second being the feminist movement and the concern with new ways of balancing work and family life. Job sharing, as an alternative for working couples, advances explorations in dual parenting, breadwinning and home-making, variations which mark increasing efforts towards resolving a myriad of personal, marriage, family and work related conflicts.

For the working couple, the job-sharing arrangement represents a structural phenomenon whereby two partners maximize *sharing* their total life with each other rather than individuals compartmentalizing it. While it is recognized that each individual has her/his own separate interests, hobbies or specialties which they pursue independent of their partner, the fact that they share marriage *and* work comes closest to a narrowing of traditional family-work gaps and to real sex-role and status de-differentiation in family and work relations. This also represents a new form of the family as an economic unit. Job-sharing couples are of particular interest in view of the fact that (1) a new dimension is now added to intimate relationships; (2) it is a viable opportunity for marriage and work to become more integrated and cooperative; and (3) as an alternate marriage and family pattern, it brings partners together emotionally and structurally while other alternatives, such as the commuting couple, often structurally separate partners, suggest that some alternatives are of a temporary solution rather than a permanent resolution of personal, family and work dilemmas.

The shared role ideology as a common denominator of all working couples has resulted in creative ways of living and working which job sharing exemplifies. The job-sharing couple struggles to maintain a balance between their unique 'gains and strains' like the dual-career family 'in which both heads of household pursue careers and at the same time maintain a family life together' (Rapoport and Rapoport, 1971). Additionally, the work sharing family which '. . . might consist in a couple sharing one and the same ordinary job, or in the wife having *one* half-time job and the husband having *another* half-time job, in the same work place as the wife, or in a different place' can provide additional insights, since 'the work-hours are synchronized, however, so that the one spouse is in the main off work while the other is on' (Gronseth, 1975, p. 7). These dual-worker patterns are part of a movement wherein working couples attempt to balance family and work responsibilities and rewards. And, within these general catagories of working couples are variations such as (1) commuting couples, where each partner pursues their career in separate locations with 'home' being in one of the two locations and a temporary home near the work site of the commuting partner; (2) now one, now the other, where individuals take turns at working (primary breadwinning) if and when opportunities exist for only one partner.

These dual-career family variations provide a model for equal participation in the home and workplace and a social structure for occupational status de-differentiation between the sexes. These arrangements are also found to increase the probability of stress in the domestic domain because the working wife's total work load is increased rather than reduced as she assumes full-time employment as well as the primary burden of domestic management and maintenance (Rapoport and Rapoport, 1971; Fogarty,

Rapoport and Rapoport, 1971). Managing the overload, even with the redistribution of tasks among various domestic helpers and services, creates a further strain on marital relations by reducing the amount of free times that couples have for social interaction and leisure-time activities. The amount of stress in a dual-career family will vary in intensity depending upon the number and quality of domestic helpers and services which they can reasonably afford or locate and the willingness of both to share equally in domestic tasks. The constraints of sex-role differentiation even in the dual-career family too often result in a 'his' and 'her' marriage (Bernard, 1972) in spite of the fact that both partners are working full-time.

The stress imposed by both marital partners working full time is particularly evident in the temporary dual-worker family where the traditional role-differentiated family structure exists and the woman has temporarily gone to work out of an economic necessity rather than a personal desire to share equally in the labor force. However, job sharing, as a result of the overall time reduction in work, along with a built-in flexibility provided by another, ultimately creates the structure for additional time which can be devoted to domestic tasks as well as leisure activities and social interaction.

In part, job sharing provides a form of resolution for the dilemmas that working couples must confront in the management of both public and domestic domains. Resolution of these dilemmas is facilitated by the nature of the rewards and advantages reported by job-sharing partners: 'more child-care time,' 'time for both to engage in parenting,' 'more research and study time,' 'more leisure' and 'free time,' 'basis of common knowledge and concern,' 'ability to concentrate on courses I teach well,' 'schedule flexibility,' 'allows for continuing education,' 'feeling of unified lives,' 'our children know their father much better than is usual,' 'because we alternate work and child care, we're well aware of the other's problems and tensions,' 'contributes substantially to our closeness as a couple.' Thus, job sharing enhances familial and personal areas which individuals and couples privately seek to develop. At first glance this work form appears to be bringing back into the family and the workplace those desired goals of egalitarian relations, dual parenting, marital satisfaction, worker morale and dignity which have eroded over time. But the economic conditions of high unemployment rates, large talent pools, affirmative actions, sex-role de-differentiation, all of which characterize job sharing, deny that this form is simply a new way of realizing old goals. Rather, for the couple who share their job, their ideology of shared roles exists in a social structure conducive to its realization. Many job-sharing couples have worked in other dual-worker alternatives and felt constrained rather than liberated. For now, job sharing for working couples is not only their most recent lifestyle, but their most equitable and flexible structural arrangement, their most rewarding experience of simultaneously managing work and family life.

Sharing a job not only provides a structure within which couples can more equally share breadwinning, homemaking and child-rearing responsibilities but a structure which provides new alternatives for employers as well. Employers are finding that job-sharing partners bring to their position the combined resources of two individuals, with creativity, experience, education and talents increasing proportionately. As a shared partnership arrangement, employers do not have to worry about vacation, sick leaves and absenteeism which leave voids in their organization and (ultimately) productivity. The flexibility of two people sharing a job reduces employers' fears of potential work overload, training of temporary part-time employees, as well as providing a structure for continuity. Employers also benefit from a built-in check and balance system for decision-making processes in a cooperative team-work environment as opposed to the competitive supervisor-employee check, a system which can foster an atmosphere of distrust and alienation. Similarly, the cooperative processes unique to *sharing* work provides the couple with a model for similar cooperative processes to operate in the home. The administrative and personnel costs of job sharing to the employer increase somewhat but the gains in flexibility, resources, morale, productivity and efficiency far exceed the costs.

Shared role ideology

The shared-role ideology is both implicit and explicit to job-sharing couples, marking a significant dimension of this working-couple arrangement. Wells College President John D. Wilson views shared appointments as a 'trend toward a new humanism reflected in the desire of young couples to share equally in the raising of their children' (Wilson, 1976, p. 3). Towards but not limited to ends such as these, New Ways To Work in Palo Alto, California, which includes job sharing as one of its programs, while originally established to increase the flow of women into the labor force, reports seeing a gradual increase in the numbers of men who are well into their first career or who, following a domestic or mid-life crisis, are actively pursuing new work options in the form of permanent part-time work or job sharing. This is consistent with some of Gronseth's findings (1975) on 'husbands' motivations for the work-sharing choice' in as much as husbands reported a 'desire to secure or develop family communality' or 'better marital relations' and 'the wish for a more purely personal fulfilment in recreation or educational activities.' While it is yet not common for men to express motivations or reasons such as these for choosing alternative means of realizing such interests and needs, a gradually growing population of professional men are actively expressing a serious interest in improving the quality of their lives by altering the full-time status of their work lives. Bernard's (1972a, p. 235) assertion that future public policy developments will necessarily find 'industry accommodating more and more to the family rather than requiring the family to accommodate to industry' is especially reflected in the expanding phenomenon of the job-sharing couple and the shared-role ideology.

The unique combination of a more actualized shared-role ideology in the home and the workplace, which job sharing encourages, especially for working couples, is only briefly mentioned in the literature. Major news media sources like the *New York Wall Street Journal, San Francisco Examiner and Chronicle* and *Business Week* have written several interesting and informational articles; local newspapers like the *Palo Alto Times, San José Mercury* and *Omaha Sun Newspaper* have likewise carried feature stories, as have individual college and university magazines featuring their 'own' job-sharing couple. A Status of Women Commission of the Modern Language Association has devoted an entire 1976 edition to *Careers and Couples: An Academic Question,* which includes a section on job sharing, and recently *Human Behavior* carried a brief article.

Systematic research on the interplay between marriage and family and personal and occupational dilemmas which working couples must organize and resolve is even more rare than the various media coverage. The social science research on these questions has been pioneered by Rapoport and Rapoport (1971), Fogarty, Rapoport and Rapoport (1971) and Gronseth (1975). Rapoport and Rapoport's in-depth study of a particular dual-career family, the Bensons, most closely approximates the job-sharing arrangement for working couples. The Bensons instituted their mutual architectural careers within their home, thereby maximizing the integration of personal, family and work relations; 'they are a husband-wife partnership at work as well as in the family.'

However, there are indications that for a variety of reasons, this is a structure and lifestyle that will suit an increasing proportion of people. While the shared family and work-role ideology characteristic of job sharing, and implicit in contemporary dual-worker models, is not implicit in previous partnerships and arrangements, the work-partnership arrangement is not new, with precursors being found in the conventional family framework, witness 'mom and pop' businesses, defined as a family endeavor but very much operationalized according to traditional sex-role and status differentiation. Outside entreprenurial enterprises, clergy and military wage earners have been dependent upon the unpaid participation and labor of wives to enhance and further their careers (Dobrofsky and Batterson, 1977; Dobrofsky, 1976). Historically and cross-nationally, in times of crisis, like war or prolonged illness, we find that the capacities, abilities and resources women use as wives are activated as managers and workers in the public domain while continuing to manage the domestic domain (Dobrofsky, 1977).

A body of sex-role and family research has focused on working wives and mothers and personal and marital satisfaction (Blood and Wolfe, 1960; Nye, 1963; Axelson, 1963; Gover, 1963; Burr, 1971; Arnott, 1972; Orden and Bradburn, 1968; Bailyn, 1971; Safilios-Rothschild, 1970; Michel, 1971). Most of the evidence concludes that working couples are more maritally content when the wife is in fact working, but working only part- rather than full-time. Findings such as these suggest that the part-time element of job sharing may be one variable behind a large-scale acceptance of this alternative for working couples. The major differences between the studies of the last ten years and job sharing, namely the spreading of a shared role and status ideology advanced by the women's movement, the swelling numbers of men choosing part-time work plus active fatherhood, and the optimum job-sharing structure within which these shared lifestyle preferences can be realized, reveal that egalitarian arrangements are only now becoming manifest and available for study.

Twenty-one job-sharing couples

Recognizing that job sharing has the potential for integrating work and family into a total social structure and provides a work option previously unavailable to the vast population of wage earners, we set out to systematically study the phenomenon of job-sharing couples. At the initiation of the study, our primary question centered on whether or not a total integration of work and family creates the ambience necessary for individual fulfilment and ultimately strengthens the bond of couples, or whether this work form is subject to the strains characteristic of the dual-worker family where the desire for more time to devote to domestic and parenting functions, as well as personal and joint leisure-time activities, are goals often expressed but rarely realized. The inquiry became more critical when we recognized the constraints of a work ethic and a society stratified by occupational status wherein the family assumes a lesser priority and women are traditionally relegated to the devalued status of family management and child care. Could the emergent job-sharing phenomenon develop as a viable alternative lifestyle and social structure which allows couples to enhance their relationship and simultaneously allows each a sense of personal autonomy?

Initially the problem was not in identifying the phenomenon to be studied but the particular population of job-sharing couples. Taking a cue from Rapoport and Rapoport's study on dual-career families (1971), we know that most dual-career couples relate socially and interact with others who are also dual-career families or other professionals. This confirms the patterns of relationships among members of the same or similar social class, education, occupation and general world view. Because of the relatively unique arrangement of dual-career and work-sharing families, it is perhaps even necessary that social relations are limited to others who are not likely to be threatened by innovative working-couple arrangements but likely to be accepting of them if not reinforcing as well. It was based on this assumption that job-sharing couples would know of others in the same particular arrangement and utilizing the grape-vine effect that the sample of 21 job-sharing couples was identified. In fact, 95 per cent of the sample knew of other couples who are sharing a job and only 5 per cent reported that they did not *personally* know others.

Beginning with a few job-sharing couples in three different occupations (clergy, academia, journalism), a letter and questionnaire were sent which explained the nature of the research interest and the unusual means of data collection upon which the researchers were dependent. This set off a chain effect whereby couples were generally able to refer to others within the same occupational category but not to others in different occupations.

As a result of the methodology, the initial study of job-sharing couples is over-representative of academicians. However, additional data obtained from job-sharing partners not married to one another tends to confirm the findings from the present sample of couples and indicate that the largest percentage of positions shared are those which have some tradition of both male and female occupation (except the clergy).

What it means to job-sharing couples

The majority (77 per cent) of the job-sharing couples feel that the shared-job arrangement has more advantages when compared to a regular job and less than one in ten consider it to have fewer advantages. Women tended to find it only slightly more advantageous than men, a reflection of the stress they feel in attempting to preserve the family in a dual-career environment or the frustration they feel from being underemployed or exploited as part-time labor. Unlike the team-work orientation of a dual-career family or the family business 'partnership,' there was no complaint that a 'buffer zone' did not exist to absorb marital and work conflicts. The nature of job sharing provides each partner with the necessary private space during either work or domestic functioning so that conflict and overlap are minimized. Since job-sharing couples mostly work separate hours and are away from home when they are working, risks of little or no personal privacy, which confront dual-career or team couples like the Bensons (Rapoport and Rapoport, 1971) are reduced and their opportunities to rotate, alternate and support one another are enhanced, a situation made possible from being 'well aware of the problems and tensions the other person faces.' However, work problems generated by one partner may become the work responsibility of the other and the potential exists for these work conflicts to get resolved at home, thereby creating marital stress as a result of job-related problems. This possibility, however, differs from ordinary cases since job-related conflicts that a job-sharing partner may bring home affect both partners and rather than scapegoating, common understanding and resolution are shared organizing goals.

While the Bensons reported that working as a team was reinforced by their marital relationship (Rapoport and Rapoport, 1971, p. 136). Compartmentalization and flexibility are essential to maintaining their totally integrated arrangement; compartmentalization to ensure necessary separations and boundaries in order to avoid too much overlap and flexibility to ensure that inevitable changes can be easily accommodated. For couples who job share, compartmentalization and separation are built in, since at any point in time, only one occupies one of the two domains and assumes responsibility for decisions during that period. At the same time, the increase in time and flexibility provides for more shared as well as independent activities in a non-competitive, low-stress environment. An academic couple who have shared a job, split a job, and had two jobs can best characterize the different processes when they write:

> With two full-time jobs, at a normal university, there is no intermingling of duties, no trade-offs; we are like any other two instructors, except that we happen to be married to each other . . . what 'spare' time we have is spent writing and haggling over chores. Gone are most of the long dinner-time discussions, replaced by harried hamburgers with an argument over who can most afford the time off to do the dishes and next week's shopping. Gone, too, the special relationship with students that our coupleness allowed for. (Schuman, 1976, pp. 34–5)

Another couple, comparing the two arrangements, comment: 'The two incomes were nice but we had no time to enjoy them,' and now, although they rarely see each other going and coming and never have lunch together, the clearest advantage has been to their family life in the form of free time on weekends and more energy at the end of the day. With two daughters, aged 7 and 11, they add:

> After ten years of relatively polarized roles we are returning to the shared housekeeping of our early married life; we choose tasks by preference and divide up the ones neither of us likes (like cleaning). Consequently our children are getting used to less rigid sex roles in the family and we are also seeing that change is possible even for middle-aged people. (Nicholl, 1976, pp. 35–46)

Stress lines: Sexism, part-time stigma, economic exploitation

Sexism

Family strains appear much less in job-sharing couples than in either traditional or dual-career families; however, external influences embodied in a sexist ideology appear to symbolize the primary lines of stress. One job-sharing partner pointed out that in the academic environment, the departmental vote is not split commensurate with the job, a situation which results in abstinence when the individuals disagree. The issue of professional identity and individuality which emerges in this context is critical. Decisions which dictate that individuals must split their vote in faculty/departmental decision-making smack of traditional sexist ideology and assumptions which surround nepotism policies. In this case, the implied assumption is that two individuals, *because* they are married, will agree on all or most issues which come to departmental vote, an unsubstantiated assumption. An academic couple remarks:

> That it is prejudice we are dealing with is implicit . . . few if any . . . have actually had *any* previous experience with a couple who shared an appointment. The argument that we might have a disruptive influence, that acting as a team our power . . . could be very great – very 'divisive' – is likewise a prejudiced opinion. (Terrebonne and Terrebonne, 1976b, p. 31)

While it is recognized that some colleagues will resist a couple having two votes, it must also be recognized that the department/university is getting two resources for the price of one (Sandler and Platt, 1973, p. 3235).

The general problem of sexist ideology in the professional world is repeated by couples as they confront such queries as '*What if* your marriage broke up?' One couple pointed out that this question probably reveals that 'most married people cannot envision themselves sharing a job with their mates' (Terrebonne and Terrebonne, 1976b, p. 5). One clergy partner reported that 'more people rely on [the] male as the *real* professional.' In the case of ministers where the wife was an unpaid extension of her husband with specific duties as the minister's wife, job sharing poses some unique identity problems, since the male must function in a reversed role as the minister's 'wife', which often means participating in women's auxiliary activities, planning church bazaars and presiding at teas.

Part-time stigma

Following sexism, the second most reported strain impacting on individuals' self-esteem stems from others' perceptions of them as less than a fully qualified member of their occupational group. The stigma of traditional part-time employment with its low status seems to prevail in interactions with members of both social and work groups. Couples also report that others tend to perceive their job-sharing arrangement as temporary and the result of the inability to find two 'regular' jobs. These perceptions and their impact stigmatize the individuals as lacking in occupational commitment or motivation; as less than fully qualified.

The part-time element of job sharing generally creates suspicion and speculation that one member is qualified for full-time employment and carrying the other who is less qualified or employable. The aura of distrust tends to persist even among employers who have reviewed the qualifications, since they are unable to fully accept that the desire to share and devote more time to family and leisure activity and to only realize one income are legitimate motivations. In part, the suspicion is real, since many of the couples who are job sharing originally sought dual-career positions (33 per cent), but are unable to find them, while others had experienced dual-career and to alleviate the strains they felt were threatening their relationship actively sought positions which could be shared.

Among the dubious attitudes encountered by job-sharing couples:

> Many feel it is 'unprofessional' – the main complaint it seems. I'm not sure what that means. It seems to have something to do with a fairly rigid notion of number of hours put in at the job, amount of time spent 'in evidence' . . . as well as, what I find to be a male definition of 'professional.' In academies the term is anything but clear. Whether more time is spent on committees than with students, or in the classroom, than on writing articles is judged positively by some, negatively by others. I can say that combined, we spend more time on committees, with students, as advisors, etc., than most members of our department.

Thus it appears that from the same professional populations which provide social support and relationships for the dual-career family, possibly also come the most serious critics and perhaps difficulties in working relations for the job-sharing couple. One job-sharing partner noted:

> Joint contracts seem to bewilder some more traditional men. That the man would share his job, and in most cases therefore also share the work at home, baffles some, threatens them too, probably.

This feeling is echoed in findings from a United Methodist Church report based on questionnaires completed by 30 of the denomination's 49 couples in the ordained ministry: 'The vast majority of those filling out the questionnaire said they feel much more acceptance from lay persons in their church than from other members of the clergy and of the church professionals' (Herron, 1975).

Economic exploitation

Supporting residual sexism and the stigma of part-time employment, we find that worker exploitation is of primary concern to job-sharing couples, a situation which could alienate them from their work group. Almost all the job-sharing couples claim that each member devotes more than half their time to the job. Their increased work load is not the result of explicit employer demands but the result of ambiguous boundary definitions and an attempt to do more than an average job to prove the benefits of job sharing to the employer. However, they also feel that the employer should recognize and compensate for the increased work, since ultimately the employer benefits. This process gets translated into a form of exploitation or belief that they are being used without the rewarding emotional or economic strokes. The majority feel that job sharing provides the employer with more than two halves and that an adjusted wage scale should be developed that recognizes the increased advantage to employers. The feeling of economic exploitation defined in terms of work produced and wages earned is the result of the marginal family income. Though most report that their total income is adequate, they feel that it is marginal and that family and individual needs could better be served with a 50 per cent increase. This accounts for most preferring to share one-and-a-half jobs as opposed to the single position. Generally, most job-sharing couples feel there is a degree of economic disadvantage which tends to foster alienation and reinforce the discrimination already felt as a result of part-time status and sexism.

The location and direction of the stress lines which confront job-sharing couples provide the key to understanding their relatively minimal impact. However while the strains generated from sexism, economic exploitation and the stigma of part-time status are very real, because they originate in and stem from an environment *external* to the couples' personal and intimate relationship, they are not as disorganizing to their internal family life as if they originated from within. For job-sharing couples, the positive gains in increased personal and leisure time, shared child care and domestic tasks and work flexibility provide unusually strong mechanisms for coping with the negative strains which originate from without. As a result, the positive gains which seemingly absorb the impact of the strains tend also to neutralize their negative effects.

Problems and resolutions

Thus, there are a number of unresolved problems and issues which presently plague the job-sharing arrangement for working couples. For the individuals as well as for their relationship, general problematic areas are economic, professional, and not least, ideological. Economically, job-sharing couples are limited by only one income while having the expenses of two workers, expenses covering clothing, transportation, conferences, etc. Many of the couples who cite this economic disadvantage recommend job expansion to one-and-a-half jobs to increase the income commensurate with the actual amount of work done, since job-sharing 'workers produce not half, but 80 per cent as much as their full-time counterparts' (Closson, 1976a, p. 36). One academic couple suggested working alternate semesters rather than sharing the work load within semesters in order to avoid the tendency for both to work more than half the job. While couples frequently note that both are working more than half of the time, or that both are doing more than half of the work, the three reasons why this situation has resulted clearly reveals where unresolved problems intersect for both the worker and the employers.

First of all, the schedule flexibility and 'freedom' of time which couples initially experience contribute to a common tendency to do a lot more than half-time employment requires. Second, couples seem to recognize their own hidden agenda in doing so much in order to oversell their case, to convince reluctant and dubious chairpersons, deans, supervisors, of the tremendous advantages rather than disadvantages of the job-sharing arrangement. Third, in their interests in being defined and treated as independent professionals, full-time expectations are the first impulse of both employers and other colleagues. The suggestion to expand the job, then, appears not only as a real possibility, as evidenced in the three cases of job-sharing couples who came to our attention, where each partner is working three-quarters of a shared position, but as more consistent with both the amount of work generated and the expectations of others.

Some working couples mention a period of reduced professional self-esteem which part-time work has forced them to confront. Concerted efforts to maintain *active* professional membership emerges as a common resolution to their own doubts regarding their full professional status. Another adjustment necessary in this context seems to center on assigning equal weight to family and community involvements, a hesitancy which tends to distort their definitions of professional self and which stems, in part, from negative views of part-time work and workers and in part from the academy's (for example) primary emphasis on research and publishing rather than community service and experience.

Ideologically, the actual operationalization of a co-operative work-family model, while enhanced by the unique structural arrangement of job sharing, is made difficult by the strong tradition of male and female domains which support the capitalist economy and Protestant work ethic. Possessiveness, in both domains fed by traditional sex-role differentiation, and competition for resources, power, status, prestige upon which a capitalist economy thrives, are properties which work against, not for, a shared role ideology and co-operative interplay between marriage, family and work relations.

Additional issues faced in a growing acceptance of the job-sharing phenomenon demand the continued interest in and willingness of employers to hire job-sharing couples. Initially there was a noticeable recurrent theme which job-sharing couples encountered, both in their applications and negotiations, making apparent where and why employers are resisting, suspicious or distrustful. This theme centers on the feeling that administrative changes are seen as nightmares, since job sharing does not fit into traditional policies and practices for paying, insuring, retiring and promoting people (Terrebonne and Terrebonne, 1976b, p. 5). Selling the new idea to the board of trustees or the president is considered not as a first but as a last resort: 'They are afraid of setting what one called "a dangerous precedent"' (Terrebonne and Terrebonne, 1976b). These reactions are found before successful precedents are established, but they continue even after positive and enthusiastic results have been demonstrated. Administrative resistance dies hard.

There are examples, however, of how some of these issues have been approached and resolved. In Wellesley College's 1975 'Part Time Faculty Policy', a variety of permanent part-time possibilities are provided (moonlighters, sunlighters, etc.), and appropriate pro-rata benefits, including salary, insurance, promotion, tenure, load and title considerations, are given. Additionally, there is now a variety of models which job-sharing couples have negotiated, and these reflect individual differences. Furthermore, an active network of communication and exchange is developing among job-sharing couples and between institutions which demonstrates a serious dedication and commitment to positive and humanistic resolutions of common problems and issues.

The administrative resistance is not, however, purely logistic in nature, as we have pointed out. Sexism, such as that which defines nepotism policies and traditional views of who is the key provider and who is the primary homemaker, also accounts for resistance of administrators to either give job-sharing couples a chance or to hire them on more than just a token basis. Administrative distrust further stems from popular beliefs surrounding part-time employment and who wants part-time work. Thus, the exploitive tendencies of part-time employment which affect the man as well as the woman require not only administrative resolutions in benefits and treatment policies, but major changes in competitive values and beliefs about permanent part-time work and toward shared, rather than stratified, role and status ideologies.

Bibliography

Anderson, J. (1972), 'A new way of sharing—one job for two,' *San Francisco Chronicle*, spring.

Arnott, C. C. (1972), 'Husbands' attitude and wives' commitment to employment,' *Journal of Marriage and Family*, 34 (4), pp. 673–84.

Axelson, L. (1963), 'Marital adjustment and marital role definitions of husbands of working and non-working wives,' *Marriage and Family Living*, 25 (May), pp. 186–93.

Bagchi, P. (1976), 'Job sharing,' *Peninsula Magazine* (4), pp. 12–15.

Bailyn, L. (1971), 'Career and family orientations of husbands and wives in relation to marital happiness,' in *The Professional Woman*, ed. by A. Theodore, Cambridge, Mass.: Schenkman, pp. 545–67.

Bem, S. L., and Bem, D. J. (1971), 'Training the woman to know her place: the power of a non-conscious ideology,' in *Roles Women Play: Readings Toward Women's Liberation*, ed. by M. H. Garskof, Belmont, C.A.: Brooks/Cole Publ.

Bender, M. (1971), 'Executive couples: reluctance to hire husbands and wives is fading,' *New York Times*, 24 October.

Bernard, J. (1972a), *The Future of Marriage*, New York: Bantam Books.

Bernard, J. (1972b), 'Changing family life styles: one role, two roles, shared roles,' in *The Future of the Family*, ed. by L. Kapp Howe, New York: Simon & Schuster.

Blood, R. O., and Wolfe, D. M. (1960), *Husbands and Wives: The Dynamics of Married Living*, Chicago: Free Press.

Blood, R. O., Jr (1965), 'Long range causes of the employment of married women,' *Journal of Marriage and Family*, (2), pp. 43–7.

Burr, W. R. (1971), 'An expansion and test of a role theory of marital satisfaction,' *Journal of Marriage and Family*, 33 (2), pp. 368–72.

Closson, M. (1976a), in 'The joys of job sharing,' *Human Behavior*, November, p. 36.

Closson, M. (1976b), 'Company couples flourish,' *Business Week*, 2 August, pp. 54–5.

Closson, M. (1976c), '. . . Job sharing,' *Business Week*, 25 October, p. 112e.

Dickson, P. (1975), *The Future of the Work Place*, New York: Weybright & Talley.

Dobrofsky, L. R., and Batterson, C. T. (1977), 'Feminism and the military wife,' *Signs: Journal of Women in Culture and Society*, University of Chicago Press, spring.

Dobrofsky, L. R. (1976), 'The wife: from military dependent to feminist?', unpublished paper presented at the annual meetings of the American Psychological Associations, Washington, D.C., September.

Dobrofsky, L. R. (1977), 'Women's power and authority in the context of war,' *Sex Roles: Journal of Research*.

Fogarty, M. P., Rapoport, R., and Rapoport, R. (1971), *Sex, Career, and Family*, Beverly Hills: Sage Publ.

Gallese, L. R. (1974), 'Two for the price of one: colleges say they get more for their money by hiring a couple to share one faculty job,' *The Wall Street Journal*, 19 April, p. 30.

Garland, N. T. (1972), 'The better half? The male in the dual professional family,' in *Toward a Sociology of Women*, ed. by C. Safilios-Rothschild, Lexington, Mass.: Xerox College Publ.

Gover, D. A. (1963), 'Socio-economic differential in the relationship between marital adjustment and wife's employment status,' *Marriage and Family Living*, 25 (4), pp. 452–8.

Gronseth, E. (1975), *Work-Sharing Families: Adaptations of Pioneering Families with Husbands and Wives in Part-time Employment*, University of Oslo, ISBN 82-570-0024-8.

Hamilton, M. (1976), 'A couple pioneers in job sharing,' *S.F. Examiner and Chronicle*, 25 April.

Herron, B. (1975), 'Report says "sexism" hurts clergy couples,' *Bread*, Iowa: Wayland.

Lobenz, N. M. (1976), 'How husbands *really* feel about working wives,' *Woman's Day*, July, p. 8.

Looker, D., and Looker, J. (1974), 'His, *Ours*, Hers,' *Sun Newspapers*, Omaha, New England, 24 October.

Looker, J. (1975), 'Woman in the pulpit: ministry family style,' *Sun Newspapers*, Omaha, New England, 9 January.

Michel, A. (1971), 'Masculine and feminine family roles: an examination of classic theory,' *Information Sur Les Sciences Sociales*, 10 (1), pp. 113–35, in *Sex Roles: A Research Bibliography*, ed. by H. Astin, Rockville, Md., NIMH.

New Ways to Work, (1976) 'Job Sharing in the Schools: A Study of Nine Bay Area Districts,' February.

New Ways to Work (1976), 'Testimony to the U.S. Senate Subcommittee on Employment, Poverty and Migratory Labor: Subject: Job sharing project of New Ways to Work,' Palo Alto, California, 8 April.

New Ways to Work (1976), 'Job Sharing: General Information Packet,' Palo Alto, California.

Nicholl, C. C. (1976), 'Will the real professor please stand up?', in *Careers and Couples: An Academic Question*, ed. by L. Hoffmann and G. DeSole for the MLA Commission on the Status of Women, first ed., pp. 32–5.

'Not just one of the Grubers' (1974), *Mount Holyoke College Bulletin*, Series 68, no. 2, November.

Nye, I. F. (1963), 'Marital interaction,' in *The Employed Mother in America*, ed. by I. F. Nye and L. W. Hoffmann, Chicago: Rand McNally, pp. 263–81.

Orden, S. R., and Bradburn, N. M. (1968), 'Working wives and marriage happiness,' *American Journal of Sociology*, 74 (4), pp. 392–407.

'P.A. group explores job sharing' (1975), *San Jose Mercury*, 21 May.

'Permanent part-time city jobs' (1976), *San Francisco Examiner*, 12 February, p. 24.

Porter, S. (1976), 'Flexitime concept gaining favor,' *San Francisco Chronicle*, 4 June.

Rabinowitz, N., and Rabinowitz, P. (1976), 'Some thoughts on job sharing,' in *Careers and Couples: An Academic Question*, ed. by L. Hoffmann and G. DeSole for the MLA Commission on the Status of Women, first ed., pp. 37–41.

Rapoport, R., and Rapoport, R. N. (1971), *Dual-Career Families*, Harmondsworth: Penguin Books.

Safilios-Rothschild, C. (1970), 'The influence of the wife's degree of work commitment upon some aspects of family organization and dynamics,' *Journal of Marriage and Family*, 39 (4), pp. 681–91.

Sandler, R., and Platt, J. (1973), 'Job sharing at Montgomery County,' *Library Journal*, 1 November, pp. 3234–5.

Schuman, D. (1976), 'Good work if you can get it: the experience of one academic couple,' in *Careers and Couples: An Academic Question*, ed. by L. Hoffmann and G. DeSole for the MLA Commission on the Status of Women, first ed., pp. 32–5.

Taylor, D. (1974), 'After the flood: Brigadier, a man "on the spot,"' *Sun Newspaper*, 10 October.

Terrebonne, N., and Terrebonne, B. (1976a), 'Sharing an academic appointment,' paper presented to the Popular Culture Association Convention, Chicago, 23 April.

Terrebonne, N., and Terrebonne, B. (1976b), 'On sharing an academic appointment,' in *Careers and Couples: An Academic Question*, ed. by L. Hoffmann and G. DeSole for the MLA Commission on the Status of Women, first ed., pp. 30–2.

Veroff, J., and Feld, S. (1970), *Marriage and Work in America*, New York: Van Nostrand Reinhold.

Wesleyan University (1975), *Part-time Faculty Policy*, Middletown, Connecticut: Office of the Provost, 15 May.

Wilson, J. D. (1976), *Part-time Faculty Employment*, Association of American Colleges, project on the Status and Education of Women, April, p. 3.

10

Separation as Support

Elizabeth Douvan and Joseph Pleck

A concern frequently voiced about dual-career marriage is that both partners having full-time careers entails a frequency of separation and a degree of separateness between wife and husband which must inevitably weaken the marital relationship. In trying to juggle the many competing demands of two careers and a family, must not the couple's own time together suffer? Will not the wife's time in her own work, or with colleagues, or in travel, detract from the marital relationship? Might not the desire of husband and wife each to advance their own careers even require living in different cities, if that is where the most desirable jobs are? And how can this kind of separation affect the marriage but negatively? Is not such a separation tantamount to ending the marriage, if not a sign that the marriage is already over?

The balance between separation and togetherness is a critical and complex issue in marital and other intimate relationships. In this paper we suggest that far from being an unalloyed stress in dual-career marriage, separation often provides a support for dual-career relationships. Separation can be seen as one of a number of 'enabling' processes in family life (Rapoport and Rapoport, 1973), processes which facilitate the involvement of family members in the larger society outside the family. In certain situations, the problem in dual-career marriages is not too much separation, but rather too little – paradoxical as it may seem. Indeed, the dilemmas faced by some dual-career couples may be soluble only through certain kinds of temporary or extended separation between the marital partners. The knowledge that separation can perform a supportive function in dual-career couples may facilitate coping with the complex tasks of integrating careers and family life.

Before presenting three case studies which illustrate the potential enabling role of separation in dual-career relationships, some general observations on separation and separateness in marriage are in order. The common view in our society has been that family life is a refuge of 'togetherness' and solidarity in a society otherwise marked by interpersonal alienation, lack of connectedness, and even conflict. This has led many to overlook how ubiquitous separation actually is in marriage. In some cultures and in some classes, long separations between husband and wife are accepted within a normative frame that makes them seem unremarkable or at least tolerable. Wealthy students from Asian cultures – both male and female – may leave a spouse (and dependent children) behind when they travel abroad for training. Military families in all cultures take for granted a certain probability of more or less extended separation. Upper-class women and their children spend winters in the sun or summers at the shore with only periodic visits from their mates. In other classes wives historically stayed behind with the children. When their husbands moved west or north to homestead or find work in the city, rejoining the husband when he had established a place in the new locale.

More generally, marriages almost universally include some separation between partners – periodic comings and goings which provide rhythm and punctuation in the relationship. The husband or wife (or both husband and wife) leave each other in the morning for work and rejoin in the evening. In farm-families the husband works in the fields while his wife works in the house and kitchen garden. Travelling sales may keep a man away from home during the week. Truck drivers, airline pilots, seamen, seasonal agricultural or construction workers and others may be away from homebase for extended periods as a normal expectable part of their situation. It is worth noting, of course, that most of these taken-for-granted separations in marriages have been those required by the *husband's* job or career. In this context, what is new about dual-career marriage is not separations, but separations induced by the demands of the *wife's* work.

The kinds of separations frequent in traditional marriage are not just tolerated or accepted, but may in fact facilitate or be necessary for the marital relationship. It is questionable whether any adult can bear total immersion in a relationship, except for very brief periods. The classic case of strain from unrelieved companionship is summed up in the very complaint of the wife whose husband is about to retire or who has recently retired. 'He's under my feet all the time' or 'He's taken over my kitchen' or 'I married him for better or worse, but *not* for lunch!' Adapted to a certain degree of separation and autonomy, couples in this position confront the need to establish new forms and styles of interaction.

Let us consider some examples of the positive use of separation specifically in dual-career marriages. We consider the use of separation to deal with dilemmas sometimes faced by dual-career couples at three different stages in their development: (1) the wife's psychological ambivalence, due to early socialization, in starting her career; (2) once having entered a career, the wife's difficulty in getting a job in her own right, and feeling that she earned it; and (3) even though having her own job, the wife's still being considered an extension of her husband by others.

The particular dilemmas presented, and the cases illustrating them, are not exhaustive of those confronting working couples. They focus on some salient ones today, particularly for women, whose role conceptions are undergoing the greatest change. The three presented serve to make a generic point, and we present them with this goal in mind.

Starting a career

Irene Barron had begun to develop an artistic talent at the end of her active career as a mother-homemaker. When her children were in high school, it became clear to her that if she was ever to let them grow into independence and at the same time maintain her own sanity, she must find an outlet for her extraordinary capacity for commitment and active work. Events of her own childhood stimulated both capacities as well as a consuming need for love and security in her attachments.

She studied sculpture with the same intensity she applied to life and within five years was producing creative and technically skilled work. She had begun to exhibit in her own community and had received a number of offers of purchase as well as some commissions. She continued to have periodic bouts of guilt and depression, in part from the loss (i.e. independence) of her children and her critical role in their lives, and in part, she felt, from the sense that she was neglecting her husband and her home as she became more and more deeply engrossed in her own work. Her husband in no way contributed to this guilt or played a reciprocal complaining role. He was a highly developed, autonomous and creative man in his own work and was thrilled for his wife in her new role and public reception. He was also in all likelihood relieved at some less than conscious level, since it was obvious that without her art, he would somehow have had to meet all of his wife's very great needs. Without either the children or her work to absorb and deflect some of their force, her commitment and energy would all have focused on him.

When Irene finally consulted a therapist, she was at the point of giving up her art in order to try to resolve her conflict. She was convinced that if she found an interest less totally absorbing, she might at least be relieved of her guilt and so avoid some of her depressive troubles.

Her therapist, on the other hand, read her depression and anxiety differently. He recognized that she was indeed in conflict but thought the source to be the issue of commitment to an independent identity. Irene had been raised in a traditional family and culture which defined identity always by attachment and service to others. And Irene had served others with devotion and enormous energy. Even her art when she began was essentially a service. An extraordinarily bright woman, she recognized the weight of her needs and developed her art in order to relieve her children and allow them their autonomy.

The problem arose really because she turned out to have real talent, to be too good at her work. So long as she was an amateur her work in no way threatened her traditional identity, her sense of herself as a dutiful wife and mother, or her femininity. But her increasing professionalism and stature, the recognition she enjoyed, contradicted in essential ways all of her early socialization. It was as though her unconscious image of her parents stood by to punish and warn her each time she experienced another success – to warn her that she might become unwomanly, to punish her for enjoying success 'all for herself' and for 'showing off.'

Her therapist read her conflict as the normal anxiety of identity formation – the fear engendered in any sensitive human being on the verge of taking a new and decisive step toward individuation, toward investment in a self which is both visible and potentially subject to criticism and responsibility. He decided to support the adventurous side of her ambivalence rather than the regressive. He would help her over the anxiety and toward growth on the assumption that once committed to the new identity, the fear and ambivalence of choosing would dissolve.

He suggested a fairly radical step to support her artistic commitment: a move to a distant city, an art center where she could consolidate her professional gains more quickly and move into the main art circles and art distribution channels. Her husband was able to go with her for a three-month period, on leave from his work, and the therapist supported a plan whereby Irene would stay on in the city for an additional nine months of intensive work. At her stage of development a year seemed a reasonable period for her to produce works and secure exhibits. Her husband would travel back and forth on weekends.

In addition to providing stimulation and professional growth, the move relieved Irene of the pressure of daily demands from her conventional conception of her role as wife and helpmate, and from the pressure of her conventional social circle, the questions and comments of friends who acted as surrogates and reminders of her parents and the socialization they had pressed on her. Almost at once the move produced results: Irene found herself able to work with an unambivalent energy she had not known since the earliest days of her anonymous amateur engagement. By the end of the year she had achieved a remarkable *oeuvre*, several invitations to enter group exhibits, and an offer from a major gallery for a one-person show the next spring.

When she returned to her home city at the end of the year, Irene had developed new work patterns, a more secure professional identity, and an enlarged capacity to assert her individuality. She is still occasionally vulnerable to thoughtless criticism from conventional friends. She is hurt even when she knows that often envy and frustration are the sources from which the criticism stems. But she is not subject to the periodic depression from internal conflict which she previously suffered, and she is, in the main, happy and feeling good about herself and her work. Her husband and children are thrilled and delighted with her and for her.

Getting work in one's own right

A second case presents equally pressing difficulties in a personal adaptation and marriage, resulting from differences of age and status. Vera and Samuel Trainer are both economists. Vera was a student of Samuel's and is some 25 years younger than he. She married him when he was a 53-year-old bachelor, adored and lionized by colleagues on his own campus and throughout the world. His colleagues and wives of male colleagues had for years considered him the most eligible bachelor they knew and expended a good deal of energy arranging parties where they introduced him again and again to attractive, bright, interesting women. Most of them had given up on his ever marrying and had settled into a kind of easy pleasure at having him in the role of family favorite. Many of his women friends tended and fussed over him like a grown-up child. His marriage to a very bright and attractive student caught them quite unprepared and not entirely enthusiastic. Vera endured a good deal of coolness, jealousy and resentment at their hands. Altogether an inauspicious beginning for her marriage, and one which forecast a number of future problems.

The main problem for Vera turned out to be very practical. She couldn't get a job that in any way corresponded to her qualifications. Nearly everyone in the field knew and admired Samuel's work and knew and loved Samuel. He could bring pressure on colleagues to hire Vera, but neither of them could in all good conscience adopt such a strategy. And none of their colleagues in the vicinity offered to hire her. Constrained perhaps in part by their resistance to the marriage, perhaps also by apprehension lest she feel they offered her a job only in order to secure Samuel's continued commitment, they did not seriously consider her even when vacancies arose for which she was superbly qualified.

For years then, Vera taught adult education courses and suffered frustration and resentment. Of course this exaggerated her problems and made it less likely that she would be offered jobs.

When Samuel approached retirement, Vera took a daring and forceful step: she applied for appropriate jobs whenever openings appeared, irrespective of their geographic location. Although no one had discussed it much, Samuel and most of his colleagues had simply assumed that he would remain in his own academic community after retirement. Still vigorous and in great demand as a lecturer and consultant, he would certainly continue as an active professional and member of the intellectual community. None of his colleagues and friends could ever imagine losing him. On the other hand none of them did anything to accommodate Vera's need for independent recognition and work – a need which she felt even more intensely when she looked ahead to 20 years of active work beyond Samuel's retirement.

She was successful in her search. She accepted a job in another part of the country, a job ideally suited to her talents and carrying all of the status and perquisites she had not previously been able to secure. The one hooker in the situation was that she would have to take the job some nine months before Samuel was free to move. After careful thought and a good deal of strategic planning, she accepted the job and the temporary distance it imposed on the marriage. At the time of his retirement, Samuel joined her in their new community.

Among the considerations that went into Vera's decision were the following: she and Samuel knew how to manage periods of separation. Over the years his consultation and lectureships had often meant being apart for a week or two at a time. With their academic schedules carefully co-ordinated they would be able to see each other for weekends once or twice a month even when she was in her new post.

Perhaps more crucial than the practical arrangements, the move carried certain symbolic advantages which were even more compelling. By keeping her husband's future relatively ambiguous – by not explicitly discussing with her new employers the fact that of course Samuel would move with her at the point of retirement, Vera was able to feel that indeed the new post was offered to her on the basis of her own ability and not simply a way of securing Samuel's services. The first year on the job without him would also give her time to consolidate her position in the university and the community independent of his reputation and power. When Samuel joined her at the end of the year, she was already an established presence and the previous imbalance in their positions was modified at least somewhat. He would continue to be in very great demand, but the primary job and anchoring was hers, as they felt it now should be.

The move has turned out to be as effective and constructive as the Trainers could have hoped. For the first time Vera works free of the frustration of under-employment. She has been more creative and productive than at any point in her previous work years. Samuel has been accepted enthusiastically by her community and has continued his busy schedule of travel and work. But he has not overwhelmed or overshadowed her in her newly autonomous status in the community.

Out of the spouse's shadow

Francine and Ralph Dimaret are remarkable people in many ways:

brilliant, talented in a variety of fields, widely travelled and read, attractive in every way. Both are intellectuals of the first rank. Being in very different academic fields, they have avoided many problems of competition and envy which they might otherwise have faced. While they will both make rare contributions to human life and culture, Ralph has a larger fame than Francine as they approach their 40s. This is due in part to his being in a field in which creativity tends to peak early and make its mark, a field in which criteria for judging significance and originality are clear and in which there is a tradition honoring contributions by the very young. Ralph has been highly honored. He is famous as well because he is among that small body of very productive intellectuals who have the energy and spirit to manage a second major intellectual and work commitment, in his case in the area of politics and public affairs. He is a radical critic of the policies of government and has consistently been a leading figure in the movements for peace and a more egalitarian society. He has attracted a good deal of attention and even notoriety.

Ralph's fame presents no intrinsic problem for Francine or for the marriage. Both of the Dimarets are highly developed individuals who have enormous respect for each other's views and work. They have different views about many things, including many of the political stands Ralph has taken. Their differences have never been disruptive because they share essential values and this strong mutual respect which is both freeing and affirming. They always managed either to work through their differences or let them stand as visible but non-divisive realities. A remarkable achievement by remarkable people.

In their middle 30s, the Dimarets for the first time accepted academic jobs which would put them on the same campus – at a state university in the midwest. In previous jobs they had always taught at neighboring schools with one or the other commuting daily. The new arrangement was ideal – it simplified and unified their lives.

It was not long, however, before the first blush wore off for Francine. The first political issue on campus found Ralph in the limelight as a leader of a small active group engaging in dramatic and effective demonstrations against the university administration. This was nothing new in their lives and was entirely within their normal expectations. What was new, however, was their geographic closeness and the response of Francine's colleagues. She was in a department considerably more conservative academically and politically than Ralph's or any department she had been in previously. Even this was no surprise to her since she had a reasonable familiarity with the attitudes of her colleagues before she accepted her post. What she had *not* counted on and was completely unprepared for was the degree to which her colleagues would judge her by her husband's actions. It was as though they were incapable of distinguishing between her and her husband. No matter how much she clarified her own position on the issues in discussion and argument with them, in the end they assumed she saw things and reacted to them exactly as her husband did. Her colleagues treated her overt behavior and declared opinions as ephemera – while her marriage and identity with her husband had the weight of some underlying truth, some more essential reality. She was blamed for his behavior and also praised for it by those few of her colleagues who agreed with him.

To Francine the praise and blame were all of a piece and almost equally offensive. The issue for this highly individuated woman (an issue about which her husband felt equally strongly) was the violation of her individuality and integrity by all those who reacted as though she were only an appendage of her husband, a pale reflection of his acts and stance. She could not seem to escape typecasting or judgment by her colleagues on vicarious grounds. After several years of trying, she came to the conclusion that she could not increase her individual impact on her colleagues, could not escape their class judgment. In order to survive as a person of integrity and to protect her marriage from the effects of unremitting frustration, she sought and accepted another job in a city university within commuting distance and has realized a successful and satisfying professional and personal life since. Geographic separation of her professional life from the overwhelming shadow of her husband's public and professional life served as a necessary support to her personal growth and to the marriage. It may not have been the only possible solution, but in the situation it was necessary, and in any event it was effective.

Separation as a solution, not as a problem

In the three cases we have presented, a temporary or extended separation played a critical role in resolving a dilemma which each couple faced as a dual-career relationship. In each case, rather than weakening the marital relationship, separation strengthened it. Though the particular characteristics or sensitivities of the individuals in each case played a part in the dilemmas the couples faced, it is important to observe that factors outside the couple created a context in which these individual characteristics generated problems which the couple had to solve.

That is, traditional female socialization results in an ambivalence about achievement that required Irene Barron to leave her family temporarily in order to crystallize her identity as a professional. It is true, of course, that many women do not need a temporary separation to allow their professional identities to develop. At the same time, though, it is also true that many women need to leave their marriages entirely in order to do so. Likewise, as long as it is widely believed that when a wife in the same professional field as a famous husband gets a job in the same geographic area, it is only because of his intercession, or because employers really want him, some wives will need to take jobs in different geographical areas in order to establish that they have earned a job through their own merit, as in the case of the Trainers. As long as wives and husbands are assumed to be proxies for each other, many couples will not be able to take advantage of opportunities to take jobs at the same institution, as in the case of the Dimarets. Until such traditional socialization and traditional perceptions are abandoned, some couples will find temporary or extended separations necessary.

While we have emphasized the potential positive functions of separations in dual-career relationships, we by no means intend to minimize the strains that separations may cause for the couple. Rather, our point is that these strains need to be put in the context of the larger dilemmas the dual-career couple often face. The couples we described have chosen a temporary or extended separation, even with all the strains it entails, in order to satisfy needs or achieve goals that could not otherwise be met. In this respect, the specific process of separation is no different from the general phenomenon of dual-career marriage itself. A dual-career marriage, as anyone in one knows, causes many strains for the couple. But the critical point is that members of dual-career couples *choose* to accept these strains as part of their fashioning a lifestyle that most fully satisfies their fundamental needs and values. In the same way, husbands and wives in more traditional marriages choose, albeit often less consciously so, to accept the strains engendered by their pattern – the trapped housewife syndrome, and the husband's breadwinner trap.

Thus, rather than viewing separation as an unthinkable option tantamount to ending the marriage itself, we should view separation as one possible kind of rationally chosen solution to the dilemmas which dual-career couples may face. It is, of course, desirable to work to alter the social conditions and perceptions generating the problems for which separation is a solution. But in the meantime, separations, temporary or extended, will continue to play a supportive and facilitative function in many dual-career relationships.

Bibliography

Rapoport, R., and Rapoport, R. N. (1973), 'Family enabling processes: the facilitating husband in dual-career families,' in R. Gosling (ed.), *Support, Innovation and Autonomy*, London: Tavistock.

11

Interdependence

Kathy Weingarten

In 1977, the numbers of married women who were employed approached 50 per cent. The two-worker family no longer represents a variant pattern but is commonplace. Also commonplace are the problems and dilemmas this employment pattern creates for those in it. This paper examines a style of interaction – interdependence – that appears to help at least one type of two-worker family – two-profession families – to cope with their exciting but demanding lives. Two-career couples in general, and two-profession couples in particular, are a particularly fortunate version of the two-worker family in that their employed activity almost always yields high income and substantial personal satisfaction.

The style of marital interaction to be described here – interdependence – is a coping strategy adopted by two people who choose to share an intimate relationship. For all two-worker families time spent away from the home reduces the time available to maintain the home and family. This results in a need, but also creates the opportunity, for an effective coping style such as interdependence. This paper will discuss the concept of interdependence, drawing on interviews conducted in the fall of 1973 in the Boston metropolitan area, with 54 two-profession couples in three different age groups, some of whom were parents and some of whom were not. The following discussion is based on content and process analysis of the taped interviews with these 54 couples. All of the anecdotes are taken from actual scenes either that I observed or that were recounted to me by the husbands and wives interviewed.

Not atypical is the following vignette. It points up the way in which a single unplanned event – a child's getting sick – draws on the available organizational skill and flexibility of the couple. The scene: Mr Jones is in his study finishing a speech he will be delivering in New York the next day, while making calls to the usual network of babysitters to arrange for someone to stay with his children for the evening. Dr Jones is talking with her answering service on the other line to ascertain how high a fever Billy Smith has, while simultaneously heating up a stew for dinner. In an hour, Mr Jones will drive to the airport, the babysitter will arrive, and

Dr Jones will meet Billy Smith and his parents at a local hospital emergency room.

Meanwhile, at Billy Smith's home, Mr Smith is calling his wife at her law office to ask her to stop off on her way home and buy a pizza so that they will not have to prepare dinner in case Dr Jones wants to see Billy that evening.

These situations arise and they put an additional stress on the already stressed two-worker family. In my research, I sought to discover how two-profession families managed to combine their work with family pleasures and responsibilities. Eighteen couples (12 of whom were parents) in each of three different age groups – late 20s, late 30s, and 50s to early 60s agreed to be interviewed jointly for two hours. Since none could have known the degree of intrusiveness of this interview, it may be assumed that couples who agreed to be interviewed felt their relationship could withstand considerable scrutiny. It may be equally fair to assume that these couples felt their lives were sufficiently successful that a researcher who presented her interest as 'understanding what enables couples to be what they choose in their adult life and how their choices affect their family and work' could learn from their experience. Both clinically and statistically, there is evidence that the couples interviewed were correct in this self-assessment. Their divorce and re-marriage rate was 7·4 per cent as contrasted with 15 per cent for professionals in general.[1] Clinically, to this observer, they seemed to fit well Burgess and Cottrell's 1939 definition of marital adjustment:

> the integration of the couple in a union in which the two personalities are not merely merged, or submerged, but interact to complement each other for mutual satisfaction and the achievement of common objectives. (Cited by Spanier, 1973, Appendix 'A'.)

These couples appeared to be successful at doing something difficult: they appeared to be intensely involved with their career and at the same time not compromising the quality of their relationships, either marital or familial.

How they managed to achieve and sustain this balance was one of the questions posed to the 54 couples in the study. With the exception of the answer, 'money,' no two couples responded alike. Despite this diversity, there was a quality to which all their explanations alluded. In fact, one sensed that they all had something in common. The quality was difficult to describe, elusive, yet in the presence of these couples, it was palpable. Words like strength, sharing, mutual respect and regard, help, co-operation, dependence, reliance, activity, energy, taking over, picking up the slack, letting go, give and take, and willpower convey aspects of the quality I noticed. These couples shared a mode of interaction that functioned adaptively in a multitude of situations. Some couples made greater use of it than others. I have labelled that mode of interaction *interdependence*.

The concept of 'interdependence' as a parameter of a relationship has not been extensively described. McClelland (1975) describes a 'feminine' cognitive style that he calls 'interdependence,' but this is different from, although perhaps involved in, the interaction made of interdependence. Whereas one is descriptive of an individual's functioning, the other is descriptive of a couple's. One reference to the concept appears in an essay by Mabel Blake Cohen (1974). She wrote:

> There is a tendency to overlook interdependency as a part of healthy human relations, both those of husband and wife and also those of people in general. . . . Perhaps a bargain is inherent in the relationship between two adequate, self-sufficient, successfully dependent adults – namely that the giving goes both ways. It would be best, then, to look for a dependency balance or equilibrium between two people. . . . In terms of dependency needs, the equilibrium must be flexible enough to allow for shifts in situations of stress. (pp. 170–1)

Theodore Lidz discussed interdependence as an aspect of the marital relationship:

> Speaking of the ideal, which reality occasionally approaches, the partners who married have each achieved an individual identity, have shown themselves capable of intimacy, and have rescinded independence for the benefits of interdependence and its security of knowing that one's welfare is as important to the partner as his own.

The psychological literature abounds with studies on helping, co-operation, altruism and support – all aspects of interdependence. But unlike interdependence, these can be parameters of many relationships. Friends support each other; strangers help each other; enemies can be encouraged to co-operate on a project of mutual concern. Only intimates can be interdependent.

Interdependence connotes more than merely 'mutual dependence' as Webster's *Third New International Dictionary* defines it. It includes the capacity to be independent in the context of an intimate relationship as well. For couples to create the conditions in their marriage such that feelings of dependence and independence can be recognized and acted upon requires considerable emotional maturity. At times one partner will feel dependent and the other will respond by becoming independent. The partners are able to meet each other's needs by balancing the emotional scale. Interdependent couples are also able to tolerate sustained periods when both partners feel and act dependently or when both feel and act independently. Both situations may generate considerable – though different – strains and stresses on the relationship. When interdependence works, there is sufficient flexibility to accommodate shifting stances frequently. Each person knows there is leeway and feels free to use it.

Interdependence is the *capacity to tolerate* all the four patterns diagrammed in Figure 4 in the varieties of contexts in which they may manifest themselves. Many couples may find themselves experiencing one or another pattern, but if it does not reflect an underlying interdependence, the pattern generates conflict. They may bicker or sulk, feel let down or abused. Rather than providing a basis for the extra margin they need to accomplish their tasks, the pattern taxes them. The marital bond is not sufficiently elastic to endure deviations from more customary ways of relating.

	Spouse	
	Husband	Wife
1	Dependent	Dependent
2	Independent	Independent
3	Independent	Dependent
4	Dependent	Independent

It may be helpful to describe couples who demonstrate interdependence in handling each of the four patterns. Consider two tense and harassed academics simultaneously coming up for tenure at their respective colleges. It is an anxiety provoking time for both and each feels need of as much care and support as possible: they feel dependent. Both would like dinner made for them; the house cleaned up; the bills paid. The couple realize this period will not continue indefinitely. If they have no children, they are able to make certain compromises, for instance in the timing and preparation of meals, that a couple with children may not be able to make. Whether they sit down and map out a long-term strategy or 'arrive' at one nightly on a continuing basis, the couple works out a way of meeting their career objectives by putting their household and relationship needs 'on hold.' The house does get messy. They are less involved with each other, and yet each wants support from the other. They do not like, but are able to tolerate, both their own neediness and the other's diminished capacity to meet it. They complain to each other and this may become the substance of their contact. They manage, in part, because they retain a firm sense of a different past and they believe that the future will be better.

If they have children, they may decide that whatever emotional reserves they have left from their work must go to meet their children's needs.

Part of their vacation money is used to hire a housekeeper to clean the house and prepare the meals, freeing them to be with their children during their leisure hours.

The situation is quite different for a couple who are secure in their careers. Whereas the first couple must accommodate to prolonged and simultaneous dependence, the second may have to adjust to simultaneous independence. The wife's career may involve travel away from home. The husband, a scientist, may be doing experiments that require him to be at the laboratory until the early morning hours. Eager to pursue the exciting developments in their careers, both would like to be away from home for extended periods of time. If they have an interdependent relationship, they will be able to negotiate this. The cost of their independence might be estrangement. Anticipating this, they try to bridge the self-imposed distance. For the wife, this may mean getting up early in order to phone her husband each time she is away from home. They share their excitement with each other, and are able to hear it without feeling left out. They acknowledge how much they miss each other. The husband drives the children to school the days his wife is away, and makes an effort to do something special – if brief – with each one. He knows that his wife will feel better about being away if she is sure the children are happy. If the couple is childless, he may take special care to keep the house neat knowing she'll appreciate his thoughtfulness.

In another situation, a couple find themselves temperamentally at odds with one another. Though the wife usually does the cooking, one evening she returns from work exhausted. She doesn't want to do anything. Nor is she able to be a pleasant companion. She has neither the energy nor the desire to mobilize herself. Her husband pours her a drink and leaves her alone with the newspaper while he improvises a meal, not wanting even to ask her what she had planned for their dinner. He responds to her feeling dependent, in this case a consequence of fatigue, by acting independently; he accepts and meets her need.

Finally, the fourth pattern reverses this situation. For example, a husband does not receive an anticipated government grant, and he has reacted by becoming mildly depressed. He is irritable and glum; he can't energize himself to get things done. His wife accepts his behavior and tries to think of things that will please him. She rubs his back and prepares meals he particularly likes. She does some of his chores – the ones she doesn't really mind – and doesn't nag him about the others. She complains a little to him, but does most of her complaining to a friend to whom she confides her wish that he'd hurry up and snap out of it.

Over the course of a couple's life together it is likely that all four patterns will occur. In some couples, their interactions may fit one pattern in the context of one issue and, at the same time, another pattern when it comes to another issue. For instance, the husband may feel dependent when discussing his worries about a promotion but within moments, act independently in attending to the children in order to give his wife time alone to read. For other couples, patterns may shift over longer periods of time, and the numbers of patterns operating simultaneously may be few. In most cases, couples do not tolerate each pattern equally well. Although there will always be personal and unique reasons why one pattern is more uncomfortable than another for someone, there are also reasons shared by most people that interfere with the achievement of interdependence. The reasons may be different for men and women.

To act independently while his wife acts dependently may fit a man's sex-role imagery well in some areas but not in others. That is, it may be comfortable for him to work on an extra project that brings in additional money in order to release his wife from several hours at her job, but he may resist and resent acting independently at other times if it means making out the shopping list or buying the children clothes. While most husbands in our society are comfortable acting independently in the first instance, they have to learn to become comfortable with the second. Yet both may be necessary to achieve interdependence. One man expressed it this way:

> I'm a lawyer in an old, established law firm. I agree with Women's Liberation and I am committed to sharing work with my wife the work that's involved in raising our family. But it's hard, let me tell you, it's hard, to explain that an important meeting with a client can't be scheduled on Thursday afternoon because I have to take my son to his piano lessons.

This 40-year-old lawyer felt isolated at his job. None of his colleagues – all men – had the kind of sharing arrangement he had with his wife. This man's stated view of the problem interdependence posed for him was that it left him open to possible contempt or ridicule. His colleagues were liable to notice that he had crossed the traditional sex-role boundary and to infer a weakness or submissiveness he did not feel.

Another man in his late 50s echoed this fear. Reflecting on years past, he said: 'I don't think people said behind our backs, "Oh, there go the Joneses, you know, the couple where the wife leaves for work in the morning and the husband kisses her good-bye".'

What he found distasteful in this hypothetical gossip was the 'total misconstruction' of what he felt they were trying to accomplish in their lives. 'You see,' he told me, 'I've never *felt* I was a Casper Milquetoast.'

These two men, due to their anticipation of social stigma, experienced discomfort acting independently in areas of stereotypically feminine endeavor. Several husbands discussed the discomfort they felt as stemming from their own internalized view of themselves as abandoning 'normal masculine behavior.'

I used to get home earlier than my wife and so it made sense for me to start the dinner. But I always felt uncomfortable. When she'd come home I'd say: 'I boned the chicken in eight minutes flat' or 'Dinner took me 20 minutes today.' I had to make it into a contest. Prove something.

What is exceptional in this instance is that the couple maintained this task allocation for several years, despite the husband's dislike of it. The hours of their respective jobs made any other arrangement less practical, more wasteful of time. The husband, with his wife's help, recognized the source of his uneasiness and decided to live with it.

Often at the same time that the husband is coming to terms with acting independently in areas for which he never anticipated taking a primary responsibility, he must face the fact that his wife is acting dependently, that she needs and wants his help. For some men – and women too – dependent behavior is difficult to accept in any adult. A man who has married a woman not despite her career but because of it may find it particularly difficult to accept an exhausted, insecure and clinging woman when he feels he has chosen a strong, active, ambitious and achieving woman. The wife's dependent behavior may evoke feelings of shock, anger or disappointment at precisely the moment she most needs his support and encouragement.

The women themselves may share their husbands' chagrin at these 'lapses.' Career women expect a great deal of themselves and often become upset and self-blaming when they do not meet their high standards at all times. A woman in her mid-30s who runs her law practice from a small room off the kitchen said she felt conflicted about her husband's feeding their young daughter dinner while she relaxed. On the one hand she was grateful that he did it, and on the other she felt she 'should be able to manage.' Many women I interviewed expressed this sentiment. One woman's husband solved the problem of where to bathe their infant son by washing him in the kitchen sink. Although she was relieved to have a solution, the wife felt she should have thought of it. Another woman, in her late 40s, found she was grateful for her husband's sympathetic toler-ance of her pre-publication anxieties at the same time that she felt guilty for 'making him put up with me.'

These women's self-chosen lives expose them to pressures, anxieties and tensions that their homemaking sisters experience in smaller, usually less sustained, doses. Career women may be anxious for months while waiting for news of a grant acceptance or job opportunity. The task of accom-modating the wife's intermittent dependence brought on by career or any other vicissitudes is a difficult one for both partners.

Men, too, have trouble accepting their dependent feelings and the fact that they may wish to act dependently with their wives. Traditionally, men have looked toward women to meet a multitude of needs – from food to sexual gratification to clean clothes. However, their behavior in their relationships with women has not been defined as dependent but as masculine. Men have had little difficulty accepting these kinds of ministrations from women. It is the perception of the need for support in other areas of their lives, such as their emotional life, that may create internal conflict.

At this time, given that few, if any, adult men have been brought up in non sex-stereotyped environments, dependence may be even more threatening to them than to their wives. Particular women may have rejected a version of femininity that includes dependence as an integral part, but when they act dependently they are contradicting their values only, not society's as well. Men transgress their own and society's views when they act dependently. Some men fight any signs of dependence in themselves and permit their wives to take care of them only under unusual circumstances – for instance post-operatively – or for short periods of time. Other men seem to have accepted their needs for periodic caretaking, although they are not comfortable talking about it. One wife confided, while her husband was out of the room, that he likes to be 'snuggled' when he comes home from aggravating meetings.

The man's dependence and the wife's responsive independence may, at times, be difficult for each. A 35-year-old architect said:

> My husband is not mechanically minded and I am. When we bought our house, I, naturally, handled all the details. It was realistic, but we both chafed. I felt angry at him for weeks and I couldn't figure out why. I was thinking things like 'Look at what this creep is making me do. What's the matter with him?'

Her husband, a professor of English, shared his perspective:

> For the first time I had thoughts like 'she *is* a castrating female,' when I'd hear her argue with the contractor. I felt very inadequate, although I haven't any interest in building and she hasn't read a novel in years!

Despite a couple's avowed belief in a woman's right and capacity to do whatever she wants, it may still be difficult to accept this in every situation. A 50-year-old pediatrician declined to be interviewed because she felt it would be 'demoralizing' for her husband, an unemployed engineer.

Unemployment of the husband is one of the situations many couples felt would be exceptionally stressful. The difficulty seemed to stem from the wife's acting independently in an area, principal breadwinner, conventionally stereotyped as masculine. Perhaps the converse of the wife's being the breadwinner is the husband's being the principal parent. This did, in fact, generate difficulty for the few couples interviewed in this situation. The wives expressed sadness over the loss of a role – *mother*, with implications of uniqueness and centrality – they had long expected to fulfil.

Rationally, they felt they had an ideal arrangement; emotionally, they felt that things were not as they were supposed to be. The husbands, all of whom enjoyed doing child care, were disturbed by their wives' reactions.

If the obstacles to interdependence are great, the rewards are even greater. Couples who have evolved an interdependent style tended to feel successful in meeting their mutual needs in both the work and family spheres. Although no two styles were exactly alike, age did seem to account for regular differences among couples in the quality of the relationship, including the quality of the interdependence. The older the couple, the more likely that independence would predominate in their relationship.

For the group in their 50s and early 60s, their careers had been well established for years. None faced externally imposed job changes. It was a time to consolidate professional skills, and experience a sense of well-being. In the family sphere, if there had been children, they no longer required the attention they once did. Often for the first time, the career cycle and the family cycle were in harmony. Couples who had been pulled close through parenting were free to establish the distance they desired. Many did, enjoying the freedom to be close or apart as dictated by their own internal rhythms as opposed to external demands. Childless couples (and in this sample none of the couples in the older group voluntarily had chosen not to bear children) no longer felt the sharp sadness of missing parenthood. They too were freer to enjoy life for what it was, not grieve for what it was not. How long their independently toned interdependence will last is impossible to determine at this point. One can speculate that the diminished health that advanced age brings will change the quality of their interdependence again.

The younger couples were intimately involved and integrally necessary to the working of each other's lives. This was true whether they had children or not. Yet it seemed that something else besides the exigencies of meshing two lives accounted for the closeness of the younger couples. It was almost as though they needed the closeness in order to cope with the psychological costs of living such complex lives. The husbands and wives needed each other to unwind, to celebrate, to commiserate, to clarify and to sympathize. The different quality of interdependence developed by the younger and older couples reflected family and work life-cycle differences.

Across ages, though, interdependence seemed to provide a critical resiliency. Not all the couples relied on interdependence to the same degree. Some couples were interdependent more of the time and in more situations than other couples. For them, interdependence proved to be the most efficient way of leading their lives. Usually these couples worked out a division of labor based on interest and skill. The jobs that no one wanted were often rotated. The task allocation frequently, but not always, diverged from a traditional, sex-role behavior assignment. Since both members of the couple *could* perform any task in any area – from cooking to dusting to buying children's shoes to talking with the plumber to getting the car fixed – if necessary, the one could take over the other's work. This often happened, whether due to fatigue, or travel, or an unexpected job demand. These couples traded flexibility for predictability; not everyone wants to or feels able to.

Other couples relied on an interdependent mode occasionally and in some instances. Their primary mode of handling and combining their complex lives took one of two forms: the traditional model or the superwoman model. Couples who organized their lives around the traditional model had a definite, fixed and relatively unchanging division of labor. The couple had been employed full time up until the point that the dual-professional involvement disturbed the desired quality of household and family functioning. At that point the woman reduced or discontinued her employment. She became responsible for the majority of household and child care tasks and her husband became responsible for providing the income. Regardless of the couple's feelings at any one particular time, the pattern of distribution of dependent and independent actions was fixed. If the wife was tired or upset from her day at home, it was still her responsibility to prepare dinner and see to the children's baths. Similarly, the husband went to work every day and took on extra assignments if financially necessary, whether he wanted to or not.

The superwoman model is similar to the traditional model in that the division of labor is fixed, as is the distribution of dependence and independence. In this case, the woman acts independently in all spheres: managing a career, the household, the children, and entertaining with relatively little besides financial input from the husband. He is dependent on his wife for services and her income is necessary to maintain their chosen standard of living.

Couples who are interdependent work hard, not only at the work they do, but also at the process of becoming and staying interdependent. It is not easy. How does interdependence happen?

The prerequisites for interdependence are the same as the prerequisites for success in every aspect of marriage: commitment and trust. Without these, couples are not able to risk as much as they must to achieve interdependence. Once both commitment and trust exist, the next step is for couples genuinely to accept that a full range of behaviors is appropriate for both men and women. The narrower the band of behavior a couple considers 'manly' or 'womanly,' the fewer will be their options in meeting the varieties of experience two careers present. A belief in people's androgynous natures is helpful. Complete emotional and intellectual acceptance of androgyny is probably impossible for anyone. However, progress towards this goal is possible if there is a constant questioning of automatic sex-role stereotyping. Biologic sex-differences are irrefutable; psychological sex-differences are not. Androgyny need not mean sameness.

It may, if that is what occurs when the two individuals let themselves feel and act exactly as they wish. But more often difference will prevail. However, the differences will be consonant with an inner rather than a societal prescription of 'appropriate' feeling and behavior.

Open communication is the second quality of a relationship necessary to achieve interdependence. Since novel behaviors are often a consequence of developing an interdependent mode of interaction, it makes sense for the husband and wife to discuss frankly how they feel about the new behavior. Some couples claim, and they may be correct, that they are able to communicate everything without putting anything into words. Somehow, as if by magic, the one always 'knows' what the other is thinking or feeling. Few are able to accomplish this. Many more think they have and learn later that they were mistaken. Most often it requires struggling to be known by the intimate other. The painstaking process of verbalizing one's thoughts and feelings is necessary. Nor is this process a one-time or one-year effort; it is perpetually ongoing. It is not always easy, and it is certainly not always fun. Sometimes hurtful things are said. Sometimes one feels raw emotions, divorced from logical thoughts. It is helpful to be able to share in this way too: the rage, the tears, the irrationality, the fears and the ecstasies. In the context of a loving, trusting marital relationship it is appropriate to confide the feelings one may have worked hard over the years to suppress. Letting go may be difficult. It may also be life-enhancing.

Finally, reciprocity – the giving and taking that M. B. Cohen writes of in the passage quoted on p. 148 – is essential for optimal interdependence. To sustain a balance of giving and taking, husbands and wives must individually assume the responsibility of monitoring their own behavior. Maintaining 'gave/got' tally sheets is not the best way to effect the balance. A genuine desire not to exploit one's partner is much more likely to result in reciprocity. Reciprocity may not be perfect during any one week, or even one year; the vicissitudes of life do not always fall equally. For some a balance may not be achieved even over a lifetime. But usually, if couples accept a wide range of behaviors in each other, communicate openly, and wish to share, a balance of one sort or another can be reached.

Interdependence proved to be an effective interactional style for the 54 two-profession couples I interviewed. Some relied on it exclusively, others only at times. It provided an on-going context within which to meet their own interpersonal needs as well as their job and family responsibilities. It seems likely that a study conducted with two-worker families would find a similar style of interaction. All two-worker couples have a pressing need to find an interpersonal strategy that helps them cope with their complex lives. Interdependence works.

Note

1 Calculated from tables in *1970 Census of Population*, 'Subject Reports: Marital Status Final Report,' PC(2)-4C, US Government Printing Office, Washington, D.C., 1972.

Bibliography

Cohen, M. B. (1974), Personal identity and sexual identity,' in J. B. Miller (ed.) *Psychoanalysis and Women*, Harmondsworth: Penguin Books.

Lidz, T. (1968), 'The effects of children on marriage', in S. Rosenbaum and I. Alger (eds), *The Marriage Relationship: Psychoanalytic Perspectives*, New York: Basic Books.

McClelland, D. C. (1975), *Power: The Inner Experience*, New York: Irvington Publishers.

Rosenbaum, S., and Alger, I. (eds) (1967), *The Marriage Relationship: Psychoanalytic Perspectives*, New York: Basic Books.

Spanier, G. B. (1973), Paper presented in the Research and Theory Section of the Annual Meeting of the National Council on Family Relations, Toronto, Ontario, October.

12

Accommodation of Work to Family

Lotte Bailyn

Every employed person is faced with the task of defining the relationship between work and family in his or her life. If one is single, without children or dependent parents to care for, this task seems relatively easy. But even in this situation the seeming ease is somewhat deceptive. Single people are very dependent on non-institutionalized relations with friends and community, and employers have sometimes found, contrary to what one might expect, that they are *less* likely than those who are married to accept geographical relocation. The complications are generally greater, however, for working couples, where each partner must resolve this issue in a way that is congruent with the other's commitments. This joint resolution is a crucial life-task for working couples, and it is the ways in which this task is accomplished that forms the focus for this chapter.

Let us define accommodation as the degree to which work demands are fitted into family requirements. Then the way each person integrates work and family in his or her life may be described by the extent to which this integration is accommodative. The extreme points of this dimension are represented by individuals who integrate family and work requirements by focusing primarily on one or the other of these areas. The highly career-committed male executive, for instance, who follows the demands of his job wherever they take him, is an example of an almost exclusive focus on work. In contrast, the wife and mother in a relatively traditional family situation, who, even when she works, is guided by family needs rather than by job requirements, is typical of someone whose primary focus is on family. The male executive is the most non-accommodative, the traditionally minded female who makes her outside interests secondary, the most accommodative. Both entail potential difficulties: the executive may find himself totally detached from his family and unable to communicate with them; the accommodative mother may not be able to give enough commitment to her work to perform effectively and get satisfaction from it. Both may be deprived of a fair and optimal chance at self-realization.

Traditional patterns have tended to approximate these extremes. The husband in our society has traditionally been minimally accommodative to family needs: his primary commitment has been to his work. And though the fruits of his labor provide for the physical needs of his family, his decisions about how best to link the family to the economy have characteristically been based solely on the requirements of his work, and have ignored the more subtle, psychological needs of his wife and children. Organizational policies have reinforced this non-accommodative stance by selectively rewarding those employees who demonstrate such a primary commitment to their work. Traditional wives' roles have been necessarily complementary: they have had to be fully accommodative, placing primary emphasis on the family. Any outside work they might do has had to be adjusted to fit this primary commitment.

But times are changing. Most of us now accept the legitimacy of women's participation in the world of work and their less accommodative orientation. And women themselves, even if their outside work was initially motivated solely by financial need, have discovered that some expression of personal competence and mastery outside the family setting often enhances their sense of well being (Barnett and Baruch, 1976). For some, of course, having to work is an indication of failure in their family situations. But when the conditions at work are right, many find that employment gives them a better opportunity to get out of themselves and to feel that they have some autonomy than the family, which may be too demanding to allow for the satisfaction of this need.

Analogously, one can find accommodative men, particularly in the middle years. These are men who resolve any potential conflict between their work and family links by re-evaluating work requirements and strengthening ties to family and community. But here, too, there are different bases for such accommodation. For some it represents the expression of a basic value: a commitment to a multi-dimensional approach to life. There are *successful* managers, for example, who at mid-career choose to reject career advancement open to them because the additional work responsibilities would entail sacrifices of family and personal involvements to which they are committed (Rapoport, 1970; Beckhard, 1972). For others, in contrast, accommodation is a response to unfulfilled expectations at work: to positions not attained and achievements not realized (Evans, 1974; Faulkner, 1974). In this case, accommodation carries with it some of the negative consequences associated with failure (cf. Bailyn, 1977).

In general, there are forces today that are decreasing the likelihood that deviation from traditional roles will be associated with a sense of failure (Albrecht and Gift, 1975). The hazards of excessive career involvement ('workaholism') are being documented; concern about equal opportunity for women in the work force is putting pressure on organizational policies that only reward non-accommodation; and more young couples are starting out their adult lives committed to an equitable relationship between them, where each has equal opportunity for occupational and family involvements (Van Maanen *et al.*, 1977; Tarnowieski, 1973; *Work in America*, 1973).

But even in a world in which options are opening up, the working couple is faced with the difficult task of managing a system based on three links, which each respond to different external and internal pressures: the *wife's work link*, the *husband's work link* and the *family link*. Each link, further, consists of a complex of elements. Work links include, at a minimum, one's orientation to the content of what one is doing, one's reaction to the organization where one is employed, and one's relations with the people with whom one works: peers, supervisors and subordinates. The family link, similarly, encompasses many different relations, including those with one's spouse, one's children and parents, and with the community in which one lives. Somehow these complex links must all be simultaneously joined in a consistent pattern. In considering accommodation in some detail, I hope to throw light on the patterns that can be forged from these three links, and on the consequences they have for the lives of working couples.

Patterns of accommodation

Each individual couple will, of course, find its own unique interrelation of these three links. But certain principles underlying these various patterns can be abstracted for analysis.[1]

A basic distinction relates to the way in which responsibilities are allocated. Some patterns are based on the principle that *responsibility for work and family is differentially distributed* between the partners. Such patterns are based on a specialization of function: though both partners maintain both family and work links, each person has primary responsibility for only one area; one is more accommodative, the other more non-accommodative. Another set of patterns, in contrast, is based on a principle of *equal sharing of responsibilities* for work and family. In such patterns, both partners have equal commitment to and responsibility for each area. Some couples who follow the principle of equal sharing of responsibilities may be quite accommodative, others may be more non-accommodative. But wherever they fall on the dimension of accommodation, the essence of such patterns is that husband and wife have the same orientation to the relation between work and family in their lives.

This distinction should not be confused with ways of describing conjugal relations according to the division of labor in performing family tasks or in making family decisions. Differentiation and equal sharing as used here refer to the relation between paid work outside the home and care and maintenance tasks within it, and the emphasis is on taking responsibility for an area, not only on task performance. Even a 'companionship' marriage, in which 'husband and wife shared both power and tasks' (Gold and Slater, 1958, p. 67) is not necessarily based on equal sharing of responsibility for both work and family.

Patterns based on differentiated responsibility

The essence of differentiated patterns is that one partner has primary responsibility for the family link and the other for his or her work link. They differ, however, from the traditional family in two important ways: first, they refer to working couples, in which both partners are in fact involved in both work and family and thus exclude the traditional situation where the wife's work link does not exist at all. Second, the decision as to which partner takes primary responsibility for which area is assumed to be based on individual negotiation and not made automatically on the basis of traditional expectations. Many of us can today point to examples of couples in which the wife's career is dominant and the husband is the more accommodative partner. And though this is not likely soon to become the modal pattern for working couples, it is differentiated in the same way as the more common case in which the wife, though committed to her work, retains a primary responsibility for the family.

The advantages of differentiation are clear. By building into the lives of working couples a hierarchy of commitments and responsibilities for each partner, the intensity of potential conflict is reduced. The process of decision-making is eased by having such built-in guidelines. Decisions ranging from the everyday (such as who stays home when a child has a cold) to the more far-reaching (where to live, for instance, and what jobs to accept) are easier to handle.

Such clarity in everyday life is very appealing. The trouble is that consequences of decisions guided by such differentiation are often irreversible. And since neither work nor family situations are static, a pattern that has worked for many years may, as one gets past mid-life, produce a sense of loss and deprivation in one or the other partner. The work-oriented or non-accommodative partner may wonder whether it was all worth while and may feel alienated from the family at a time when meaningful personal ties take on great importance. Or, the family oriented partner may suffer from the greater work success or satisfactions of other people (particularly, perhaps, the spouse) resulting not from any differences in ability and interest, but based merely on a forced reduction in total commitment to work (see, e.g., Bailyn, 1964). Though such consequences are less likely to be disturbing if real differences guide the initial allocation – differences in age, or in abilities, or in temperament – differentiated patterns, which are one-sided by definition, entail these risks.

Patterns based on equally shared responsibilities

In patterns based on the principle of equal sharing, both partners have the same commitment to each area and share equally the responsibilities of each. This situation represents the ideal lifestyle for many young couples, who embark on their adult lives in a more equalitarian atmosphere than was true even a decade or so ago. Such 'symmetrical' patterns, where there are 'no monopolies for either sex in any sphere,' are increasingly visible (Young and Willmott, 1973, p. 275) and have been shown to be associated with an increased enjoyment of activities by both husband and wife, particularly the latter (Rapoport *et al.*, 1974). They are supported also by analysts who feel that a meaningful and satisfactory life in a complicated world necessitates fully androgynous sex-roles (Rossi, 1964; Rowe, 1974). But the principle of equal sharing, because it does not provide the guide-lines implicit in differentiation, requires more attention, more energy to make it work. In general, it confronts the working couple with a more complex situation. Its potential rewards are high, but the difficulties of implementation cannot be ignored.

Without some way of reducing complexity, patterns based on equal sharing may produce, particularly at certain stages of life, a serious condition of overload (cf. Rapoport and Rapoport, 1976).[2] Such a stage is likely to be reached in the late 20s or early 30s – often near the seven-year 'danger' point in a marriage (Chilman, 1968). Both families and work careers go through identifiable stages, which vary according to the degree of involvement they require. The difficulty at this vulnerable point in life stems from the fact that stresses in both cycles characteristically peak then: both seem to require maximum attention (Wilensky, 1961; Troll, 1975). Sociologically and biologically this is the optimal time to have young children, hence family demands are maximal. It is also the time in their employees' lives when employing organizations tend to make decisions about future placement, decisions at least partially based on the degree of involvement and commitment to work demonstrated by the employee. 'I live two lives,' one male teacher in his early 30s explained; 'one is pro-fessional and one is as a family man. The two lives are neither mutually exclusive nor fully compatible. . . . The main problem . . . is to establish a healthy balance between the two lives in order not to sacrifice my family life *now* to build for a better family life in the future. The other half of the conflict is, of course, not to sacrifice my career opportunities *now*. . . .' And if the wife is also working, the task of establishing a 'healthy balance' is even more complicated.

How can a working couple reduce the complexity of a pattern based on the principle of equal sharing, particularly at such a vulnerable stage? Three general strategies are available. The first is perhaps the most obvious: *limitation* of both partners' involvement in one or the other area.

Which area is chosen will depend, primarily, on how accommodative the couple is. Couples who believe in the principle of equal sharing and tend to be non-accommodative find it useful to lessen the family demands on them by having no children, or only one child. In contrast, if the couple tends to be accommodative, they lower their career aspirations and intentionally step off the fastest promotion tracks. Both decisions, of course, may have irreversible, lifetime consequences, but by being taken jointly and shared equally, they are less likely to become sources of deep regret or acrimony. Certain environmental supports, moreover, which are increasingly seen, also help limit the demands of each area. Day-care centers and housing developments with shared central facilities introduce in a new context some of the advantages of the extended family. And on the work side, there are flexible time schedules, reduced time requirements and shared jobs.

A second approach to reducing complexity might be called *recycling*: a shift in the staging of work and family events (Rapoport and Rapoport, 1976; Strober, 1975). This too is a strategy that combines individual decisions and external forces. Its main effect is to reduce the likelihood that periods of maximum demands in the family and work areas overlap. Medical advances in diagnosing and treating prenatal abnormalities and wide use of adoptions – both of which allow families to have children at a later stage than is now deemed optimal – help couples shift the periods of peak demands in the family cycle. Analogously, the increasing incidence of successful 'second careers' (Sheppard, 1971; Sarason *et al.*, 1975) shows that periods of maximum work involvement can fruitfully be postponed to later stages in one's life. Organizations, of course, will have to stop considering age a legitimate ground for employment discrimination if such recycling options are to be widely available. But age stereotypes that constrain flexibility in employment patterns are already being challenged: by the necessity to retrain employees of all ages because of technological change; by the entrance of older women into the labor market. Ideally, the strategy of recycling allows one to make up at a later stage in life the limitations one imposed earlier. And though limitations once imposed can never be fully recovered, by balancing the consequences for the two areas, this strategy is particularly useful for couples whose orientation is near the middle of the accommodation scale.

A final strategy to reduce complexity introduces *segmentation* into each partner's life by strengthening the boundaries between family and work: by compartmentalizing each area so that one does not have to deal with family and work issues at the same time. This strategy seems, at first, counter-intuitive, as it has been seen as a shortcoming of our contemporary society to have such a degree of segregation between work and family life. However, by allowing one to express one's commitment to each area sequentially instead of simultaneously, it eases the strain of equal-sharing patterns. Leaving one's work at the office is the day-to-day expression of this strategy. Work concerns are attended to in one place during one period of time; at home, in contrast, during the rest of the day, family needs take absolute priority. Geographical separations, including long-distance commuting, which have been described in other chapters in this book (chapters 7 and 10), often emerge, unexpectedly, as mechanisms for allowing one of the partners to concentrate completely on work for one period of time, for instance during the week, and revert to total immersion in the family the rest of the time, as on weekends. Another innovative expression of this strategy is to apply it to a lifetime. This is not new to women, of course; indeed, sequential involvements were for many years deemed optimal for working wives and mothers. What is new is to apply this strategy to *both* partners of a working couple. Paternity leaves are a social innovation that begins to make such life planning possible.

Whatever the time frame, however, the essence of this strategy is to reduce complexity by strictly segmenting work concerns from family concerns.[3] A comparison of two occupations – the college teacher and the engineer in industry – will emphasize the point. College teaching is often assumed to be an ideal occupation for one or both partners in an 'equal-sharing' family. Formal responsibilities are minimal: daily time schedules have great flexibility, the location of work is often immaterial, there are long periods with no formal duties at all. How much easier to mesh such a work schedule with a working spouse than that of the engineer who has to be away from home every day from at least nine to five, 50 weeks of the year. Of course there is truth in this, but an important fact is often overlooked. The engineer, despite the rigid time schedule, can segment work and family concerns, whereas the college teacher finds this much more difficult. Academic norms put heavy pressure on a professor to keep up with a field, to do research, to write, often to consult – activities that are much harder to segment than the formal requirements of a job. And, indeed, research in America has shown that the permeable boundary between work and family that exists in the academic profession tends to outweigh the advantage of flexible schedules: male professors in the USA are considerably less accommodative than male engineers (Bailyn and Schein, 1976).

The above strategies indicate some of the ways working couples can reduce the complexity of patterns based on equal sharing of responsibilities. But there is still another issue, that goes beyond complexity: such patterns maximize the potential conflict between the work links of the two partners because they are based on the principle that these two links are given equal weight. This kind of conflict is much less likely to occur in differentiated patterns, where the two work links are ordered into a hierarchy of importance.

One way of dealing with this potential conflict is for the couple to participate in a *joint venture*, thus reducing the two work links to one.[4]

Obviously such an approach is only possible if both partners do the same or highly complementary kinds of work, though some joint ventures – such as small family businesses – require such general input that a wide variety of couples can participate. This is an intriguing way of eliminating potential conflict between the work links because it is the only one where achievements at work are truly additive, where both partners can limit their aspirations and involvements with work and yet both reap the benefits of career success. Despite this appealing quality, however, there are also drawbacks. Most obvious is the fact that the two partners' skills and interests may not mesh in the requisite way. Moreover, joint ventures require a degree of intimacy and lack of personal competitiveness that is beyond the capacity of some people. Finally, it is more difficult, in a joint venture, to reduce complexity by segmenting work and family concerns. When Bertrand Russell and his wife started a school, for instance, it was a most successful venture for everyone except their own children, who evidently suffered from the lack of segmentation in their parents' lives (Tait, 1975). But even here inventive solutions are possible. I know one couple who in remodeling their home to house a business, specifically did not build an inner door to connect the two halves of the house. There were two entrances and one had to go outside and re-enter when moving between family residence and place of work.

Joint ventures, where feasible, can meet the needs of 'equal-sharing' couples, whether accommodative or non-accommodative. Other ways of dealing with the potential conflict between the two work links are more suited to either an accommodative or a non-accommodative orientation. Indeed, for very accommodative couples the whole issue of potential conflict between work links may never arise since all work decisions are made on the basis of the requirements of family. And though such couples may find it more difficult to meet their needs for accomplishment in the external world, the simplification of the issues involved is obvious.

An entirely different way of responding to the potential conflict between the partners' work links in patterns based on equal sharing is particularly suited to the needs of more non-accommodative or career-oriented couples. It is almost the exact opposite of the joint venture and rests on an *independent* relation by each partner to his or her work. In this approach, a favorite of young ambitious couples starting their joint lives at the same stages in their work careers, the decision is initially made not to resolve any conflicts between the work links, but to adapt to them. In other words, each partner follows his or her optimal career path and the couple adapts to the consequences that ensue. Full-time nannies, whether they come in the form of grandmothers, au pair girls or day-care supervisors, and long-distance commuting are examples of such adaptive mechanisms. Such a strategy capitalizes on the autonomy of each partner and is not likely to work well with people who are more dependent on others. Quite the contrary, it probably is most successful when used by those who have some difficulty in forming intimate relations. Indeed, from the findings on commuting couples (Ngai, 1974 and ch. 10), it seems that some of these marriages survive only because of the separation imposed by the commuting. Such marriages obviously are different from those that succeed on the basis of a full sharing of lives. But for the people involved they may represent a very satisfactory alternative to complete separation.

Thus, patterns based on equal sharing of responsibilities confront couples with a number of issues to be resolved. Two have been discussed here – level of complexity and potential conflict between the two work links – along with some of the strategies that can be used in dealing with them.

Any of these patterns, whether based on differentiated or equally shared responsibilities, may be successful in providing each partner in a working couple with satisfactory family relations and with rewarding work. But the probability of success will be different for each depending on the personal characteristics of the partners (temperament, needs and abilities), the way in which these mesh with each other, and such other factors as family structure and the circumstances of work. The success of an 'equal-sharing' pattern, for example, depends on similarity of personal characteristics in the partners – at least on the major issue of how they balance the relation between work and family in their lives – whereas a differentiated pattern is likely to be more successful if these orientations are different, though complementary. Similarly, some patterns will fit better with some family structures than others. A couple pursuing an independent pattern based on equal sharing, for instance, will probably find life difficult if they try to have many children. Indeed, unless there is at least one fairly accommodative partner, the decision to have children at all, or more than one child, can lead to a serious condition of overload.

As to the constraints imposed by the requirements of work, we have already alluded to the fact that different occupations will fit better with certain patterns than with others. There is one general point, however, that must be made. The path to most higher positions in organizations – whether technical, professional or managerial – is premised on a career progression that primarily fits the life of a non-accommodative person – indeed, in some cases it actually requires the services of an accommodative spouse (Papanek, 1973). Though we now question the assumed 'naturalness' of this situation and some beginning has been made in loosening the organizational policies that propagate this assumption, it is a 'fact' of organizational life, as we know it today, that working couples cannot ignore. It is unlikely, for instance, that any of the highest occupational positions in our society will soon be held by an accommodative person. For anyone aspiring to such a position, therefore, the appropriate differentiated pattern is more likely to be successful than one based on equal sharing of responsibilities. Indeed, research has shown that even professionally trained wives of highly career-oriented husbands find it difficult to work in their professions (Bailyn, 1973), and, if they do, the couple's marital satisfaction is likely to be low (Bailyn, 1970; Rapoport and Rapoport, 1976).

What this means is that though working couples have many options in organizing their lives, these options all involve costs. It is the understanding of what these costs are that may allow us to set in motion processes that will reduce or modify them in the future, and help us minimize the toll taken by uninformed life choices.

The dynamics of accommodation

All of this has so far been described in a fairly static way, as though the task of fitting the demands of work to family requirements were resolved once and for all at a single point in time. But accommodation is not, in fact, a static state. On the contrary, it reflects a continuing process of response to the changing demands of work and family and to the successes and failures experienced in each area.

Each adult, upon embarking on the twin tasks of starting a family and entering the world of work, has some idea of what he or she assumes the relation between work and family will be. This initial set of assumptions is based on the culture in which the person lives, on the example of the parents' pattern, and on some sense by each individual of important needs and abilities. Such an initial orientation may be more or less accommodative. When it is based on the assumption that life will revolve around family concerns, the person's career and family decisions, expectations and reactions to experience are guided by a highly accommodative orientation. At the other extreme, if one assumes that work will be the focus of one's life, one's orientation is very non-accommodative and one will make different decisions and have different expectations and different reactions to experiences. As long as these experiences are relatively congruent with the initial orientation, it is unlikely to be much modified. If, however, results turn out to be unsatisfactory or not to fit initial expectations, then a process of re-evaluation may be set in motion which will change the initial orientation.

Sometimes this initial orientation is primarily shaped by external pressure: by society or parental models. If a person's own capacities, needs and interests are not accurately reflected in such a 'stereotyped' orientation, dissatisfaction is likely to result. A woman who remains a housewife because she assumes that that is what she ought to do, even though her talents go in very different directions, is likely sooner or later to suffer from this discrepancy between her initial orientation and her talents. She may find that a re-evaluation toward a more non-accommodative orientation will lead her to seek employment outside of the house and result in a more satisfactory life for her and her family. Or, a man who works very hard to become president of his company because his father is a successful business man and expects it of him, may discover that successive promotions do not bring the satisfactions he anticipated. He may realize that his needs are not met by rising in an organization's hierarchy and may find that a redirection toward a more family-centered lifestyle provides more meaningful rewards for him. In both these examples, a re-evaluation is set in motion because of a discrepancy between an initial orientation based on externally imposed role expectations and what might be called a person's 'real' self.

But even if an initial orientation is consonant in essential aspects with a person's 'real' self, discrepancies may arise. The most general pressure toward re-evaluation stems from the failure of primary expectations. Frequently these are 'disconfirmed' expectations, but re-evaluations can also be stimulated when initial expectations are exceeded. A middle manager, for instance, who receives an unexpected series of new job challenges is likely to become very work-oriented; one who fails to receive a desired promotion is likely to become more oriented to his family (Evans, 1974). Similarly, a symphony player who fails to achieve a desired seat in a top orchestra learns to value the slower-paced life provided by the community orchestra in which he is employed (Faulkner, 1974).

Whenever there is a discrepancy between primary expectations and actual experiences, a pressure for change is built up. New orientations that respond to this pressure are likely to be based on a more realistic understanding of the circumstances in which one lives, and hence more likely to lead to satisfaction with one's life. Sometimes, of course, circumstances can be overwhelming. But occasionally even such traumatic events as the loss of a job or the death of a spouse can force a re-evaluation which in the long run will lead to a more satisfactory fit between one's orientation and the circumstances of one's life.

At other times, however, a change in life circumstances or in basic values may transform a good fit between orientation and experience into a discrepancy. In fact, any major discontinuities in one's life may make a re-evaluation of initial orientations necessary. Thus, a group of happy, family-centered, 30-year-old women were found to be maladjusted at 70 when their children had left home and were inaccessible; in contrast, a group of unsatisfied 30-year-old housewives who changed their basic orientation and became 'work centered,' were found, at 70, to be very contented (Maas and Kuypers, 1974).

Personalities vary, of course, in their capacity to react constructively, and sometimes no re-evaluation occurs despite very great discrepancies between orientations and life experiences. This may happen when a person's investment in the initial orientation is so strong – for reasons probably related to the early development of the personality – that change is seen as impossible. An example might be the man who continues to work hard and long, ignoring most other aspects of life, despite the fact that he no longer gets any enjoyment or sense of accomplishment from his work; or the woman who finds her life empty after her children are gone, but is unable to reorient herself to activities outside the home. Such unresolved discrepancies between orientations and experiences may on occasion lead to depression or to other symptoms of distress such as alcoholism (cf. McClelland *et al.*, 1972; Wilsnack, 1972).[5]

There are also external constraints to change. Most organizations, for instance, put pressure on their employees to stay highly involved in their work, and feel that something is wrong if they become very accommodative. But as long as not all the work that must be done is intrinsically challenging, and as long as organizations must find a place for their 'plateaued' employees (Goode, 1967), such secondary accommodation may actually be more beneficial than disruptive to the enterprise as a whole (Bailyn, 1977). Indeed, we know that it cuts down on employee turnover (Getchell, 1975).

More important to the concerns of this paper, however, is the impact of a change in orientation on a *couple's* pattern of adaptation. What happens when one partner changes and the other doesn't, or when both change but in opposite directions? Although we do not know very much about this yet, it seems that some of the satisfactions of the later years stem from the fact that reduced demands from work and family permit couples to share their lives more equally (Deutscher, 1964). Thus a change by one partner of a differentiated couple in the direction of the other one is likely to be adaptive. Sometimes, though, there is a criss-crossing of previous orientations (Gutmann, 1973; Lowenthal *et al.*, 1975): the accommodative partner becomes so non-accommodative and the non-accommodative one so accommodative, that a reversed differentiated pattern may result.

There is also, of course, the possibility of radical change. The second career, for instance, may require relocation and certainly requires re-establishment. Though sometimes this takes the form of a joint venture and therefore does not lead to direct conflict with the spouse's work link, some re-adaptation between the partners will always be necessary. Even more disruptive to established couple patterns are the re-evaluations that sever the family link entirely. Divorce at all stages – even after decades of living together – is becoming more prevalent (Glick and Norton, 1973), and we are only beginning to understand how men and women in different circumstances adapt to it (see, e.g., Weiss, 1975). It is interesting, however, that some analysts see divorce as the 'chance of a new lifetime' for mothers (Brown *et al.*, 1976), and others suggest that divorce (severing the *family link*), as a response to an unmanageable situation, is no more extreme than the severance of the *wife's work link*, which happens when a competent and committed professional wife resumes the traditional family role when she has a child (Holmstrom, 1972).

Obviously, there is much still to be learned about these dynamics. Some couples' patterns will change during the course of life-development, others not, depending on the experiences encountered and the capacity of the partners to adapt to new circumstances. Clearly the goal is neither change nor stability for its own sake, but change or stability in order to achieve a workable resolution of family and work demands for each partner that meshes well with the needs of the other.

All indications point to an increase in the number of working couples in the future. As more people attempt to work out the problems of such double careers they will exert pressure on employing organizations to reconsider some of the policies that now restrain available options. But the complications introduced by superimposing two work links on the family link will remain. And though innovative resolutions will emerge in dealing with different degrees of accommodation in the partners, the potentially successful combinations are not limitless. It is not possible for both partners in a working couple to do everything. Some choices will always be necessary: regarding work, perhaps; or family; or both. Let us hope that the continuing study of the situation faced by working couples will enable them to make these life choices more rationally. The more accurately the reality of their situation is perceived, the more likely it is that their chosen lifestyle will be successful.

Notes

1 Detailed accounts of the lives of working couples are available in Rapoport and Rapoport (1976), Holmstrom (1972), Lein *et al.* (1974).
2 Bebbington (1973) points out that the stress involved in these patterns may replace, and be preferable to, stress stemming from an unsatisfactory resolution of conflict between desired and actual roles by one of the partners of a dual-working couple.
3 Pleck (1975) points out that the boundary between work and family is 'differentially permeable' for men and women. Segmentation, therefore, requires that men stop the spillover of work into family areas, and women the spillover from family to work.
4 Some of the issues involved in such joint ventures are examined by Epstein (1971) in her investigation of husband–wife law partnerships and by Rapoport and Rapoport (1976, pp. 95-150) in their discussion of a husband–wife partnership in architecture.

5 Turner (1971) offers the intriguing hypothesis that since external constraints to divorce are decreased in dual-career households (particularly those patterned on a principle of equal sharing), personal and individual compatibilities are more determining of marital stability or dissolution in these cases. This hypothesis gets support from an analysis of couples in communal households, where external constraints to divorce are even less (Jaffe and Kanter, 1976).

Bibliography

Albrecht, G. L., and Gift, H. C. (1975), 'Adult socialization: ambiguity and adult life crises,' in N. Datan and L. H. Ginsberg (eds), *Life-span Developmental Psychology: Normative Life Crises*, New York: Academic Press.

Bailyn, L. (1964), 'Notes on the role of choice in the psychology of professional women,' *Daedalus*, 93, pp. 700–10.

Bailyn, L. (1970), 'Career and family orientations of husbands and wives in relation to marital happiness,' *Human Relations*, 23, pp. 97–113.

Bailyn, L. (1973), 'Family constraints on women's work,' *Annals of the New York Academy of Sciences*, 208, pp. 82–90.

Bailyn, L. (1977), 'Involvement and accommodation in technical careers: An inquiry into the relation to work at mid-career,' in J. Van Maanen (ed.), *Organizational Careers: Some New Perspectives*, London: Wiley.

Bailyn, L., and Schein, E. H. (1976), 'Life/career considerations as indicators of quality of employment,' in A. D. Biderman and T. F. Drury (eds), *Measuring Work Quality for Social Reporting*, New York: Halsted.

Barnett, R. C., and Baruch, G. K. (1976), 'Women in the middle years: A critique of research and theory,' Radcliffe Institute.

Bebbington, A. C. (1973), 'The function of stress in the establishment of the dual-career family,' *Journal of Marriage and Family*, 35, pp. 530–37.

Beckhard, R. (1972), 'The executive you're counting on may be ready to mutiny,' *Innovation*, May, pp. 3–10.

Brown, C. A., Feldberg, R., Fox, E. M., and Kohen, J. (1976), 'Divorce: Chance of a new lifetime,' *Journal of Social Issues*, 32, pp. 119–33.

Chilman, C. S. (1968), 'Families in development at mid-stage of the family life cycle,' *Family Coordinator*, 172, pp. 297–310.

Deutscher, I. (1964), 'The quality of postparental life: Definitions of the situation,' *Journal of Marriage and Family*, 26, pp. 52–9.

Epstein, C. F. (1971), 'Law partners and marital partners,' *Human Relations*, 24, pp. 549–64.

Evans, P. A. L. (1974), 'The price of success: Accommodation to conflicting needs in managerial careers,' unpublished Doctoral Thesis, Sloan School of Management, M.I.T.

Faulkner, R. R. (1974), 'Coming of age in organizations: A comparative study of career contingencies and adult socialization,' *Sociology of Work and Occupations*, 1, pp. 131–73.

Getchell, E. (1975), 'Factors affecting employee loyalty,' unpublished Master's Thesis, Sloan School of Management, M.I.T.

Glick, P. C., and Norton, A. J. (1973), 'Perspectives on the recent upturn in divorce and remarriage,' *Demography*, 10, pp. 301–14.

Gold, M., and Slater, C. (1958), 'Office, factory, store—and family: A study of integration setting,' *American Sociological Review*, 23, pp. 64–74.

Goode, W. J. (1967), 'The protection of the inept,' *American Sociological Review*, 32, pp. 5–19.

Gutmann, D. (1973), 'Men, women, and the parental imperative,' *Commentary*, December, pp. 59–64.

Holmstrom, L. L. (1972), *The Two-Career Family*, Cambridge, Mass.: Schenkman.

Jaffe, D. T., and Kanter, R. M. (1976), 'Couple strains in communal households: A four-factor model of the separation process,' *Journal of Social Issues*, 32, pp. 169–91.

Lein, L., *et al.* (1974), *Final Report: Work and Family Life*, Cambridge, Mass.: Center for the Study of Public Policy.

Lowenthal, M. F., Thurnher, M. P., and Chiriboga, D. (1975), *Four Stages of Life*, San Francisco: Jossey-Bass.

Maas, H. S., and Kuypers, J. A. (1974), *From Thirty to Seventy*, San Francisco: Jossey-Bass.

McClelland, D. C., Davis, W. N., Kalin, R., and Wanner, E. (1972), *The Drinking Man*, New York: Free Press.

Ngai, S.Y.A. (1974), 'Commuting as a solution to geographical long-distance limitation to career choices of two-career families,' unpublished Master's Thesis, Sloan School of Management, M.I.T.

Papanek, H. (1973), 'Men, women, and work: Reflections on the two-person career,' *American Journal of Sociology*, 78, pp. 852–72.

Pleck, J. H. (1975), 'Work and family roles: From sex-patterned segregation to integration,' paper presented at the meetings of the American Sociological Association, San Francisco, August.

Rapoport, R., and Rapoport, R. N. (1976), *Dual-Career Families Re-Examined*, London: Martin Robertson; New York: Harper & Row.

Rapoport, R., Rapoport, R. N., and Thiessen, V. (1974), 'Couple symmetry and enjoyment,' *Journal of Marriage and Family*, 36, pp. 588–91.

Rapoport, R. N. (1970), *Mid-Career Development: Research Perspectives on a Developmental Community for Senior Administrators*, London: Tavistock.

Rossi, A. S. (1964), 'Equality between the sexes: An immodest proposal,' *Daedalus*, 93, pp. 607–52.

Rowe, M. P. (1974), 'Prospects and patterns for men and women at work,' *Child Care Reprints IV*, Washington: Day Care and Child Development Council of America, pp. 91–118.

Sarason, S. B., Sarason, E. K., and Cowden, P. (1975), 'Aging and the nature of work,' *American Psychologist*, 30, pp. 584–92.

Sheppard, H. L. (1971), 'The emerging pattern of second careers,' *Vocational Guidance Quarterly*, 20, pp. 89–95.

Strober, M. H. (1975), 'Women and men in the world of work: Present and future,' paper presented at the Aspen Workshop on Women and Men: Changing Roles, Relationships and Perceptions, August.

Tait, K. (1975), *My Father Bertrand Russell*, New York: Harcourt Brace.

Tarnowieski, D. (1973), *The Changing Success Ethic*, New York: Amacom.

Troll, L. E. (1975), *Early and Middle Adulthood*, Monterey: Brooks/Cole.

Turner, C. (1971), 'Dual work households and marital dissolution,' *Human Relations*, 24, pp. 535–48.

Van Maanen, J., Schein, E. H., and Bailyn, L. (1977), 'The shape of things to come: A new perspective on organizational careers,' in L. W. Porter, E. E. Lawler and J. R. Hackman (eds), *Perspectives on Behavior in Organizations*, New York: McGraw-Hill.

Weiss, R. S. (1975), *Marital Separation*, New York: Basic Books.

Wilensky, H. L. (1961), 'Life cycle, work situation, and participation in formal associations,' in R. W. Kleemeier (ed.), *Aging and Leisure*, New York: Oxford.

Wilsnack, S. C. (1972), 'Psychological factors in female drinking,' unpublished Doctoral Thesis, Department of Social Relations, Harvard.

Work in America (1973), Report of a Special Task Force to the Secretary of Health, Education, and Welfare, Cambridge, Mass.: M.I.T. Press.

Young, M., and Willmott, P. (1973), *The Symmetrical Family*, London: Routledge & Kegan Paul.

Prospects

Twelve contributors have applied their research experience, each to the consideration of a particular process confronting working couples today. In so doing, they have built up a picture of many of the key issues that transcend different social environments and situations. They have also specified many of the issues that are specific to situations such as cultural differences (Safilios-Rothschild/Dijkers); phase of the family cycle (Bailyn, and Douvan/Pleck); external linkages to the world of work where many occupations are highly demanding (Handy, and Gowler/Legge) and make it a particularly uphill, cross-grained effort to establish this pattern of work and family life.

Research from other countries, such as France (Andrée Michel), the Soviet Union (Karchev and his colleagues) and Finland (Haavio-Mannila), has confirmed that many of the key generic issues apply in other settings as well, despite specific differences of cultural, economic and political context. There is everywhere the problem of finding two jobs of commensurate attractiveness to the marital partners; working out interpersonal agreements on life-goals and strategies which will be felt to be equitable as well as viable; handling unconventional asymmetries of resources, prestige or power when they arise, without undue disruption to the intimate marital relationship; choosing child-care resources and arranging things so that they can be made to work without harm to the children; working out accommodations with the world of work and interdependence in the performance of domestic obligations.

These discussions have made it plain that the phenomenon of working couples – strains and all – is not an aberrant or freakish phenomenon that has developed as a peculiarity of a particular time and place. The dual-worker family has world-wide relevance and legitimacy, though it is not a simple, unitary phenomenon. It is a highly complex, multifaceted and dynamic type of family structure. The presentations lay out some of the main issues involved and describe experiences of working couples in dealing with them. But before more is suggested, it is useful to consider some of the gaps in our available knowledge. For an adequate understanding of issues and their solutions confronting working couples, it is important that these gaps be filled.

Four gaps

We point to four gaps which we see as priority areas in the search for further knowledge.

One gap is in the occupational linkages of families as seen from the *employers' perspective*. Many of the researchers have highlighted the difficulties confronted by the marital partners in attempting to find appropriate work and to adapt their work schedules to the requirements of being a partner in such a family, and of the ramifications for the other partner of difficulties experienced, conflicts aroused, overloads entailed. Much less is known about employers', colleagues', clients' and others' capacity to adapt their requirements to the workers' own wishes and needs. Most work-roles and organizations have been defined and structured as though the family were not there, except in the background, after hours and compliant to the primacy of the work-role. It is difficult for individuals or families to change a work situation. Though many individual spouses may wish changes to occur in order to accommodate family interests, they may also feel uncomfortable or insecure about being *the one* to be pushing for change. In such a situation the difficulties may be particularly acutely felt. It is, therefore, especially important to learn more about the employers' perspectives on these issues of changing occupational roles – so that they may be detached from the personal definitions of the situation.

At present, a frequent situation is one in which husbands indicate a readiness to be 'fair' about taking domestic responsibilities but feel reluctant to ask employers for latitude to do so for fear of losing ground in the competitive situation of the job. Husbands may actually ask their employers and receive the reply 'impossible'. The idea that workers should be primarily responsive to the job is so ingrained that it is impossible for many employers to envision change. There may, therefore, be an actual collusion between employers and employees to see any alteration of the status quo as out of the question.

What is needed is a more open-minded, innovative approach to the problem of the structure of work. We know from some early experimentation in certain industries and branches of the Civil Service that there are situations in which part-time work or flexible working hours or job-sharing arrangements can be successful and advantageous. In such situations there is a demonstration that unorthodox working arrangements are not only possible but may serve the goals of the work organization.

In situations where this is not seen as advantageous, it remains to be demonstrated whether this is because of a conservatism of managerial outlook, or because of real differences in the requirements of different work tasks.

It is necessary to keep an open mind on both sides on this, and to be ready to find that in fact it is more costly in sheer economic terms to accommodate work organizations to family interests. The issue would then be one of working out some form of cost-accounting in which economic gains and losses are combined with non-economic ones to arrive at a conclusion. A multi-dimensional approach allows for the consideration of values other than economic productivity, though real-life situations vary in how realistic such an enlightened perspective may be. The requirements of cash-flow and productivity are more salient in times and places of economic hardship or survival risk.

The second gap is in the parent-child relationship, from the *child's perspective*. Several of the papers have considered issues confronting parents, e.g. the working family team in their analysis of the division of responsibility between fathers and mothers; Kathy Weingarten in her discussion of the complexities of implementing the concept of marital interdependence, and Mary Rowe in her discussion of parents' choice of child-care options. Less attention has been given to the child – not only the effects on the child, but the child's part in the process. Research to date has concentrated on the global question of whether there is evidence that the child is harmed, for example, if the mother goes out to work. Having established a 'not proven' situation, to replace the previous one which implied a generally applicable hazard to child health, we are now confronted with the questions of 'under what conditions' is the hazard increased or decreased? And, 'what are the consequences for the relationship' of choosing one option or another? Clearly child health is at risk if there is neglect or abuse; and children as well as adults can play a part in the process of producing undesirable outcomes. A child who is irritable, or defective or difficult in various ways for whatever mixture of biological and environmental reasons, may provoke reactions which produce a vicious cycle of mutual rejection and provocation. This sort of pattern is as well known for the child's participation in it as are the more adaptive patterns, such as the child's smile stimulating an affectionate response in the parent, the child's playfulness stimulating reciprocal responses and so on. The issue of how parent-child relationships evolve in a particular valued direction is more complex, and little is known about the child's part in it. Some researchers, e.g. Bronfenbrenner and Lois Hoffman, have given attention to the question of parents' values in the child-rearing process: do they want to produce warm and loving co-operative children (as the Russians seem to do) or independent, competitive children (as the Americans seem to do)? Parents' values in relation to their children are becoming clearer. Children's attitudes to their parents have received much less attention, except in problematic situations.

We seem, in our society, to have swung from an earlier attitude that children were to be seen and not heard and that one did not regulate one's life for them, to the more recent child-centered attitude whereby the total responsibility for the child's mental health and development was assumed to be in the hands of the parent, usually the mother. In fact, children are more or less interested in their parents' affairs, have a greater or lesser involvement at different points in their development and the important point seems to be for parents to remain sensitive to children's attitudes and needs, and to recognise that they change. From one of the few studies that have been done on children's attitudes toward changing parental roles, Coutrot and Ormezzano, a French research team, has found that within reasonable limits it is not so much what the parents do in relation to child care as how they do it. Children want their parents to be happy, to feel personally fulfilled and not guilty, martyred or trapped in either their domestic or their occupational roles.

A third gap is in relation to *sexuality*. Here again, there seems to be a backlash against the idea of equal opportunities for men and women. One idea that is expressed in opposition to all this equality, and to women having equal work opportunities, is that women will become harder, more aggressive and bossy – less desirable; and that the men will become emasculated in the relationship. Sex has been portrayed, for such couples, as at best a businesslike and expedient affair, and at worst a fiasco, with the males often impotent. It is assumed that the meaningful intimacy of a trusting and tender relationship will disappear. Contemporary publications contain illustrative accounts on this theme. But, there are many methodological problems and the case for the validity of this picture is far from established. Sexual problems exist in our society on a wider scale than can be attributed to the impact of women's working. And working couples are capable of sustaining a normal (if not a 'super') sex-life. But more systematic work is needed to specify the part work or its absence can play in interfering with people's sex-lives, whether we are looking at working couples or at the marriages of people in specific occupations, such as management, the professions or long-distance lorry driving.

Having a spouse who is out and about amongst other people may either make him or her more attractive, or it may present new barriers in the relationship. At present this is an area of ideological and counter-ideological assertion, coupled with selective anecdotes. More knowledge is required about this topic before anything definitive can be said about the idea that the wife's working has a direct impact on the couple's physical sexuality.

The fourth gap is in *theory*. One might ask, 'who needs theory?' This is a descriptive book. It provides insights into facets, issues, processes. Knowledge is something that seems to be wanted by many people, whether or not it has the further effect, as some would hold, of enriching the quality of effectiveness of the way couples live their lives. But theory has a relevance that goes beyond academic interest. It is not only academicians designing research projects who use theories, but policy-makers (whose decisions are of vital importance to working couples as they seek to evolve new patterns of relationship with their social environments) and also couples themselves. Examples can illustrate the use of theory at these different levels. Take the issue of coping with the stresses and strains involved in operating the dual-worker pattern. Many of the researchers note that the couples they studied experienced heavy strains and overloads, and often asked themselves whether the stresses are worth it. To some extent their answers (and the answers of those who are concerned for them) are based on their individual capacities to tolerate (and even to seek) stress – but to some extent they are based on a theory. If the theory is that we are at a stage in social evolution toward a more symmetrical arrangement between the spouses' family and work roles – as Young and Willmott (1973) have argued in their book, *The Symmetrical Family* – then the difficulties are seen as transitional. Particular couples may feel encouraged by the notion that they are pioneers, and that history is with them. Which of these pioneers is able to manage the complexity of their transitional situations with its lack of resources and social supports, its personal doubts and interpersonal conflicts is another matter. If, on the other hand, the theory is a socio-biological one, such as that espoused by Lionel Tiger and his associates, the couple's effort to cope with their predicament is seen in a different perspective.

Lionel Tiger, and to a different degree many of the biologically oriented anthropologists, sociologists and ethologists, have argued that it is un-natural for women to seek roles which are demonstrably masculine. Their conception of what is demonstrably natural for males and females has been the record of animal and human evolution. They have recently produced a further case in point, namely the Israeli experiment with kibbutz life. Tiger and Shepher, an Israeli sociologist, have argued that this experiment began with an egalitarian conception of sex-roles, but after a wholehearted attempt to implement the idea it has produced communities in which the women do the laundry, cooking and service occupations, like teaching and social work, while the men manage the enterprises as well as doing most of the heavy agricultural work. They argue that this vindicates their theory and imply that such experiments are wasteful because they are doomed to failure.

Policy makers and couples who adopt the first theory are helped in con-fronting stressful situations by the idea that they are in the vanguard of history, pioneers. Policy makers and couples who reject the idea of dual-worker families as a valued model, assume that for most people the happiest solution is the conventional one, with men and women sticking to traditional roles.

To some extent the co-existence of these two theories constitutes a modern manifestation of the old 'nature-nurture' controversies, and as such is subject to uses and abuses and biased selection of data to rationalise pre-determined positions. Nevertheless, it is important not only to academics, but to people generally to have these debates continue, to produce and display evidence on all sides of the complex topics concerned, and to assume that people both wish to have and are able to use available evidence and argument.

Theories are useful in explaining experience, and in guiding actions which can affect experience. There are, of course, many theories of varying degrees of complexity and comprehensiveness. Two theoretical approaches that seem useful and worth cultivating to improve our understanding of the specific situations encountered by dual-worker families are the *dilemma* approach and the *exchange theory* approach.

The dilemma approach focuses on the importance of decision-making in dilemma type situations. Couples of the type described here seem to face a life-course punctuated by dilemmas of one kind or another, and the available research suggests that the capacity to confront such ambiguous and conflict-laden situations and create satisfactory resolutions to them is a crucial element in sustaining the viability of the pattern.

The exchange theory approach complements this in that it provides a framework to encompass gains as well as losses in any optional resolution of a life dilemma. Also, this approach allows for a cumulative effect through time. Sussman (1975) writes:

> The availability of options results in tradeoffs in the exchanges of inter-acting individuals. In the quest for ends ranging from survival to maximal self-actualization and achievement, individuals implicitly or explicitly consider their investments and costs in the situation and 'risk' a response which will provide a maximum profit at least cost or loss. Some situations may require taking a loss in hope for a future gain, and compliance is the process in this particular tradeoff. Briefly, negotiation and bargaining for power and position with concomitant esteem and status in relational systems are continuous exchange processes.

This exchange theory approach has had a wide demonstration of its utility as an explanatory framework for social-psychological as well as economic phenomena – from the times of Max Weber through contemporary writings of people like Peter Blau. Marvin Sussman considers that the *equity* concept (Rapoport and Rapoport, 1975) is fundamental to modern exchange theory, implying 'a sense of fairness in the distribution of rewards based on one's contribution to the interaction . . .' (p. 567). Negotiations and re-negotiations are constantly required to attain and sustain the desired level of satisfaction. The contributed papers have illustrated both the process and some of the possible techniques for optimising results.

But more research and experimentation is required; for which this framework is likely to prove useful.

Futures

The tensions and dilemmas of working couples may turn out in the long run to be a transitional phenomenon in the evolution of symmetrical families, or they may be a relatively permanent structural feature of this particular pattern. What is unlikely is that they will prove to be a freakish phenomenon, produced by temporary conditions of our current economic circumstances.

Any discussion about where our future lies should, in our view, be firmly rooted in a pluralistic conception of contemporary society and a willingness to recognise the complexity of social change processes. We do not, as a society, march in an orderly column toward a clear goal of a desired future, though there are elements of that. Conversely, we do not become preoccupied with particular family types – like dual-worker families – as aberrant types, straying from the straight and narrow path of social progress.

What we have is a congeries of different sub-groups; a change process that is subject to backlash and bottlenecks, to turbulence and complexity. Within this the family cannot be the area of calm and stability that it is often portrayed ideally to be. It, too, is subject to similar human processes of tension, competition, confusion and negotiated settlements as are other, less personal areas of life. But, within the family there are some potential points of strength. Within this small and personal structure people can construct patterns which equip them to deal with areas of turbulence in their lives. The family itself may also be turbulent, as we have suggested. For some people it may be the job that is stable and the family that is turbulent, for others the reverse. But the family is more accessible to personal construction and management.

Changing family structure, as many of the contributors have shown, is not, however, as easy as it might seem. The domestic division of labour has been spotlighted as a problematic bottleneck in the change process. To deal satisfactorily with it – to reconstruct and manage new forms of family structure with a feeling of equity and satisfaction – new structures of relationship between families and work organisations are likely to be developed. Given the plurality of human preferences in the family this is likely to involve the fostering of flexible work arrangements of various kinds. Two elements seem crucial in considering family futures. First, there should be many possible futures, not one.

Second, there should be a recognition of the possibility of making our own futures. We can 'wait', like Godot, for the future to happen to us. But, though we cannot determine it altogether, we prefer to try to make our own futures. Families have the advantage of being of a size and scale that is amenable to management by individuals, communicating, taking decisions, implementing values. While it is true that many people may feel, in the face of the family's intensity of emotional forces, that they are more capable of managing large organisations than their own families, we suggest that there should be, and will be, an increased capacity to deal with non-rational elements in human relationships, and that this will help with intimate relationships in the family. Indeed, families can provide the feedback of human experience to complement and counterbalance the emphasis on rationality, instrumentality and impersonality provided by educational and occupational institutions.

The protean family

The kind of family that we envision as best suited to be a model for the future is not exclusively the dual-worker family. This is one option among many. Nor is the symmetrical family or any other *the* family the model. Rather, we suggest as a guiding concept the *protean* family. The protean family is not a single type at all but an idea of variation and change in family structure to suit on the one hand the makeup of the individuals, and on the other the situation that they confront – in their internal life, in their occupational and community life, and in different phases of their life-cycle.

Conventionally, when a lady married her 'knight in shining armour' and withdrew from her maidenly pursuits to 'build her nest' and have a family, the image was one of 'happily ever after', constancy, unchanging devotion and undiluted love. The conception suggested, of the protean family, is one that conveys a different image. Rather than becoming a rigidly routinised conventional family, such a couple may entertain ideas of altering their structure when the children are thought to be ready to be left with others, or when the parents feel that the balance of benefit amongst themselves and their children would alter for the positive if the young mother pursued other interests. Protean orientations would allow for the possibility that a husband might like to withdraw from his work, or reorganise it in such a way that he could spend more time in domestic care responsibilities while his wife, if she should wish and feel the need for it, went out to work. The idea of work sharing would be no more binding than the idea of a conventional division of labour, and the protean couple would test and alter their optional choices and arrangements as they are found not to be suitable, or no longer to bring optimal satisfactions and a sense of equity.

The protean family is not, on the other hand, a 'chameleon' family of superficial bonds and commitments. Rather is it an *enabling* family, assisting its members to adapt and to overcome the various structural binds and constraints that impede them in their quest for personal satisfaction in a social framework rather than by withdrawal (Rapoport and Rapoport, 1973).

There are certainly many barriers, constraints and difficulties that have to be overcome to establish such a family orientation. Many of them have been documented in the contributed papers which serve to chart some of the difficulties associated with constructing, managing and altering dual-worker families. But, as the contributions have shown, there are not only barriers and pitfalls, threats and hazards. There are rewards and satisfactions, and there are signs that things may, after all, get better for those who choose to depart from what has been laid down as the single right and proper way of organising one's life.

What are the signs warranting optimism? First, it would seem that there are other forces at work in the occupational system and elsewhere that may be moving congruently to those which have been advocated to clear the bottlenecks required for the protean family to function. These forces include the critique of largeness in bureaucratic organisations ('small is beautiful') and of the dehumanisation of productive technology ('quality is working life') and of the environment.

Efforts to rearrange occupational task groups into smaller, more flexible and more humane groupings should work in the direction of recognising that workers are people, they have families, and men as well as women may have domestic interests which can be articulated with the requirements of the workplace.

Second, there is a swing of the pendulum away from being as child oriented as we have been in the past as a society. This does not imply a diminution of interest in children and in making arrangements that will enhance child development and avoid child neglect. Indeed, there is an argument that *less* concentration on children may be better for them in many instances. Children need to be less passive, less dependent. More active participation as responsible members of family and social grouping may facilitate their own development as well as providing help for their parents who wish to do more to meet their own needs as well. The findings of Coutrot and Ormezzo, that children really want their parents to be satisfied and fulfilled, is relevant here, and it is quite likely that we shall be in for a period in which a new image of children emerges, one that emphasises their capacity for independence and co-operation rather than their psychological fragility.

Perhaps the bond most likely to hold the protean family together as it shifts its structure to accommodate different situations and family life-cycle stages is that of *friendship*. Friendship does not happen automatically, any more than does love or respect. It is present in all humans as a *potential*, but it needs cultivation. It has been neglected in our society. Its application to the democratisation of the family and the humanisation of the workplace is needed and wanted – and it is therefore likely that the family will both contribute to and benefit from any move toward cultivating friendship and conviviality in our society.

Bibliography

Blau, P. (1964), *Exchange and Power in Social Life*, New York: Wiley.

Bronfenbrenner, U. (1977), *The Experimental Ecology of Human Development*, Cambridge, Mass.: Harvard.

Coutrot, A.-M., and Ormezzano, J. (1974), *Chers Parents*, Paris: Laffont.

Haavio-Mannila, E. (1972), 'Convergences between East and West; tradition and modernity in sex roles in Sweden, Finland and the Soviet Union,' XII International Family Research Seminar, Moscow.

Kanter, R. M. (1976), *Work and Family in the United States*, New York: Russell Sage.

Karchev, A., and Emelianova, K. L. (1970), *Brak: Ideal i deistvitelnost*, Moscow: Akademiia Nauk.

Michel, A. (1970), 'Wife's satisfaction with husband's understanding in Parisian urban families,' *Journal of Marriage and the Family*, August.

Rapoport, R., and Rapoport, R. N. (1973), 'Family enabling processes: the facilitating husband in dual-career families,' in R. Gosling (ed.), *Support, Innovation and Autonomy*, London: Tavistock, pp. 245–64.

Rapoport, R., and Rapoport, R. N. (1975), 'Men, women and equity,' *Family Coordinator*, vol. 24, no. 4, pp. 421–32.

Sussman, M. B. (1975), 'The four F's of variant family forms and marriage styles,' *Family Coordinator*, vol. 24, no. 4, pp. 563–76.

Tiger, L., and Shepher, J. (1976), *Women in the Kibbutz*, Harmondsworth: Penguin Books.

Young, M., and Willmott, P. (1973), *The Symmetrical Family*, London: Routledge & Kegan Paul; New York: Pantheon.

Index

DATE DUE

1987	DEC 0 7 1995
	1